PR That Works

Paramount Press

Praise for Steve Turner and PR That Works

"I worked with Steve Turner and Solomon/Turner for over a decade and can think of no one better to write about their storied career and the creative PR strategies he utilizes to help clients reach success. We utilized Steve's expertise to formulate a public relations strategy for Northwestern Mutual-St. Louis where none had previously existed. His firm creatively planned and executed a brand-building campaign to build awareness and bring the financial advisors of Northwestern Mutual into prominence with the local media. They helped land coverage in top tier local publications and helped with planning and assistance of our special events. Steve is a good thinker who cares about what you care about. His efforts were instrumental in helping our office reach a top ranking among all Northwestern Mutual offices nationwide. I highly recommend any student or veteran PR practitioner read this book and apply many of the lessons to grow and advance their careers." **—John Qualy, Managing Partner (retired), Northwestern-Mutual-St. Louis**

Steve and Solomon Turner don't just open doors; they create opportunities. One memorable example was a breaking cybersecurity story where, within less than an hour, Steve had me prepped and on-air at a major TV station. That single day turned into eight media appearances across television and radio, something I never would have accomplished without his guidance and relationships. Beyond media exposure, Steve has been instrumental in helping us gain recognition through numerous awards and accolades, raising our visibility and credibility in the industry. His professionalism, strategic thinking, and unwavering commitment have been a driving force behind much of our public presence and brand reputation. **—George Rosenthal, President, ThrottleNet**

"Steve and Solomon Turner were instrumental in helping us launch a full-scale public relations campaign to build the brand of Brian Tracy Seminars and Peak Performance International. They helped us create a campaign where none had previously existed. Their efforts helped attract large crowds to our seminars and had a huge impact on our success. I am excited that a chapter on our relationship is included in the book. One that will be read and studied by those wishing to grow their careers in PR."
— **Dan Brattland, President Peak Performance Int'l**

"Steve Turner's superpower is helping companies enhance their brand and gain business through targeted PR campaigns. He has helped Cohen Woodworking dynamically increase name recognition and build relationships across the nation. His book, PR That Works, brings together his years of experience and expertise, and can help anyone enhance their knowledge and application of PR strategy." — **Nate Cohen, Co-owner, Cohen Woodworking**

"As President of OfficeWare I worked with Steve Turner and his firm for many years. I can't say enough good things about the success of his PR efforts. It probably was our highest marketing return on investment. Over the years we appeared in numerous newspapers. I was interviewed and published on more than one occasion. We even made the NBC Nightly News. Steve always worked closely with our team. He was persistent in helping us seek out public relations opportunities and he established great rapport with the local press." — **Rick Maxwell, President, OfficeWare (sold to Konica Minolta)**

REAL STRATEGIES. REAL CAMPAIGNS. REAL RESULTS.

PR THAT WORKS

STEVE TURNER

PARAMOUNT PRESS

PR THAT WORKS

ISBN: 979-8-9931927-0-3

LCCN: 2025921522

© 2025 Steve Turner, Chesterfield, MO 63017 U.S.A.

All rights reserved. No part of this book may be reproduced in any form without permission in writing from the publisher. Reviewers may reproduce short passages as quotes within a review.

All trademarks and brand names referenced in this book are the property of their respective owners. Their inclusion here is for illustrative and educational purposes only and does not imply any endorsement or affiliation.

Printed in the United States of America.

PUBLISHED BY
PARAMOUNT PRESS
CHESTERFIELD, MISSOURI

This book is dedicated to my partner in business and life, Shelly Solomon, who has been with me throughout this exciting journey.

Acknowledgments

Many thanks to my editor, Cindy Mosher, who provided great insight and guidance throughout this effort.

Last but not least, I would like to thank my wonderful and generous parents, the late Beverly and Herman Turner, who provided my siblings and me with every chance to succeed in business and life.

Contents

Praise for Steve Turner and PR That Works
Acknowledgments ... iii
Contents ... v
Foreword ... vii
Introduction ... ix

Part I Principles—The Nuts and Bolts of PR ... 1
1. PR Frontlines—Warfare with Words ... 3
2. Rethink PR—It's Not Publicity ... 7
3. Plan the Attack ... 11
4. It's Not an Ad, It's PR ... 15
5. PR Is More Effective Than Advertising ... 19
6. Building an Objective to Drive Results ... 23
7. Media Relations: The Inside Pitch ... 27
8. Media Relations: The Strategy ... 31
9. PR Pros Aren't Liars ... 37
10. The PR Big Top: Juggling Negativity ... 39
11. Strike Zone: Managing the Media ... 45
12. Swimming with PR Sharks ... 51
13. PR and Sales: Myth vs. Reality ... 55
14. Thought Leadership ... 59
15. Podcast Power ... 65
16. Are You a Lion or a Gazelle? ... 71
17. Wordsmithing: A Superpower ... 73
18. The Press Release: Why It Still Matters ... 77
19. Mastering Response Time ... 81
20. Oscar Worthy Award Strategies ... 85
21. Choosing The Right PR Firm—Be Selective ... 89
22. PR: The Digital Calling Card ... 95
23. Recruiting PR: Taking a Company from Good to Great ... 99
24. The Power of the Subject Line ... 103
25. Measuring What Matters ... 109

26 PR Drives Value and Brand Equity	115
27 Agency Lifeblood: Winning New Clients	119
28 Embrace the Future	125

Part II Campaigns That Work — 129

Campaign #1 The Million Dollar Baseball	131
Campaign #2 Spotlighting an Icon: The Original Jeeps	135
Campaign #3 A Pig's Tale—One Penny at a Time	141
Campaign #4 Dialing Up: An Underdog Story	145
Campaign #5 Hanukkah, Oh Hanukkah	149
Campaign #6 The Law of Attraction	153
Campaign #7 Dot-com Daze	157
Campaign #8 A Woodworker Crafts Success	161
Campaign #9 Game On—From Newcomer to Market Leader	165
Campaign #10 Breaking Barriers: The Legendary Contracts of Jackie Robinson	169
Campaign #11 SARS Wars	173
Campaign #12 Celebrity Driven Success	177
Campaign #13 Barks & Bites	181
Campaign #14 Legends on Wheels	185

Part III Craft Masters: Inside the Toolbox—Insights from the Best in the Business — 191

Michael Smart	193
Taryn Scher	197
Natalie Bushaw	203
Dave Collett	209

Elements for Success: The PR Campaign Top 10	215
For the Road Ahead	219
Resource Guide: Featured Companies & Helpful Links	221
About Steve Turner	223

Foreword

"I've known Steve since college where we were close friends and collaborated on impactful projects that guided young men through their college entry experiences. Our friendship continued after college, helping us channel opportunities and build trust in our business relationships as well.

Steve and Solomon Turner have done an excellent job helping us expand our brand both locally and nationally. Through their expertise, we have won awards and secured extensive media placements in print and television.

Steve and his partner Shelly Solomon help create character in people as well as brands, resulting in successes all around.

They bring a wealth of experience in public relations, and this book goes beyond a biographical memoir—it delivers valuable lessons to help anyone elevate their PR strategy, execution and results." —**Howard Laiderman Chairman/CEO Veterans Home Care**

Introduction

"It's up to us to save the world."
—Patrick Jackson, PR executive

I once attended a Public Relations Society of America seminar featuring the late Patrick Jackson, one of the 20th Century's most widely known and respected public relations practitioners. He won numerous awards, teaching and guiding others toward where the profession was heading. This included the strategy, techniques, and philosophy needed to get there.

That day, Jackson spoke about the ongoing conflict in the Gulf War. He described how the United States was trying to educate Iraqis suffering under tyranny and oppression. The military dropped leaflets and other materials as they prepared to overthrow Sadam Hussein.

The goal was to showcase democracy and prepare them for a better life.

Highlighting this, Jackson emphasized that as public relations practitioners, it is up to us to save the world.

These words have stuck with me over the years. Public relations professionals are highly skilled in their craft. By utilizing proper strategies and messaging, they help shape public opinion, settle conflicts, win elections, launch new products, and build businesses.

Jackson's words provided a north star to seek constant improvement and learn new skills. I have followed this mantra in various forms for over three decades and continue to do so today.

At the start of my career, mass media consisted mainly of TV, radio, and newspapers. It has since evolved to include a variety of social platforms such as Facebook, TikTok, Instagram, LinkedIn, YouTube, and X (formerly Twitter)—as well as podcasts and other digital media.

As audiences spread across a variety of platforms, the art of public relations—reaching key stakeholders and customers—has never been more challenging or more interesting. Today, words and images emanate quickly, crossing platforms and time zones in an instant. Yet many of the core strategies, themes, and practices that were important early in my career are still in vogue today.

The crafting of key messaging and delivering it across the right channels can help build businesses, bring societal issues to the forefront, stir political action, and change the world.

The art and science of how those messages are created and disseminated is what public relations is all about.

I wrote PR THAT WORKS in part as a memoir, but mostly as an educational tool. It details the lessons learned from over 30 years as a public relations practitioner—many acquired the old-fashioned way, through hard work, discipline, hustle, trial and error, failures, and successes. These lessons are as applicable now as they were then.

The book outlines the key nuggets of creating and developing campaigns in various forms for corporations, small businesses, and well-known personalities. It has been written in three separate sections: Principles: The Nuts and Bolts of PR, Campaigns – PR In Action, and Craft Masters – Inside the Toolbox: Insights from the Best in the Business.

The first section contains the nuts-and-bolts aspects of PR, covering strategies and techniques to consider and apply for any relevant campaign.

The next section contains campaigns turned into action—actual work we orchestrated in conjunction with our clients. I greatly appreciate all the outstanding companies, causes, and individuals we have worked with over the years, and thank them for allowing me to tell their stories. Many of these campaigns can serve as case studies and can be referenced for future planning.

The third section features interviews with some of the top professionals in the industry. I wanted to provide insights from a broader perspective and am thankful for their input.

With that, here are PR workings drawn from over three decades in the public relations industry. The high points and low points along the journey.

Study them. Apply what you can to your practice and career. And most of all, enjoy them.

Whether you are a student pursuing a career in public relations, a new practitioner, or an industry veteran, I believe you will find value in these tools. Ones that can help you cut through the clutter and find a higher level of success for you, your business, your client or your agency.

Who knows, you may even save the world.

Part I
Principles—The Nuts and Bolts of PR

The practice of public relations has never been more challenging. It is tech driven across various digital platforms, AI enhanced and tasked to produce measurable outcomes in an endlessly changing media landscape. Yet the nuts and bolts behind successful campaigns remain unchanged. What follows are foundational strategies designed to support both newcomers and seasoned professionals—a toolbox to build better campaigns, help grow client businesses, and enhance your career.

1
PR Frontlines—Warfare with Words

It's been said that "Business is war without bullets." In public relations, that war is fought with words.

Words have meaning.

Words have influence.

Words shape perception.

Depending on its intent, wordcraft can initiate or escalate conflict. Conversely, it can reduce tension and even eliminate a hostile situation. Words can change history.

President Ronald Reagan said, "Mr. Gorbachev tear down this wall". Signifying the end of the divide between East and West Berlin and the cold war with the USSR.

Dr. Martin Luther King's famous "I have a dream" speech at the Washington Monument was a call to action for racial equality.

Winston Churchill guided Britian and the allies to victory in World War II. He inspired the British people in 1941 during the heat of conflict when he delivered his "Never Give In" speech, often termed "Never Give Up." Churchill told his audience, "...this is the lesson: never give in, never give in, never, never, never, never-in nothing, great or small, large or petty—never give in except to convictions of honour and good sense. Never yield to force; never yield to the apparently overwhelming might of the enemy."

More recently, the words "Thirsty after you catch on fire?" headlined a viral TikTok video featuring the Stanley Quencher Tumbler. The video showed how the tumbler survived a fire, and even the ice did not melt. It was not planned but the words and video generated 84 million views. The follow-up video by Stanley's President generated another 32 million views and turned the Stanley Cup from a niche product for campers to a must have mainstream item resulting in millions of dollars of sales and revenue, as well as brand awareness, for the company.

In a business sense the right phraseology can help an unknown company enter the competitive "battlefield" and build its brand. It can help a company find its voice among dozens or hundreds of "assailants" all fighting for a share of the market. Public relations properly applied can "arm" a sales team and marketers with the proper ammunition needed to win their individual battles.

In today's digital world, the right combination of words and images can help a business plant its flag atop the corporate mountain top. Consider campaigns for well-known brands. Most started with limited name recognition but utilized creative ways to generate momentum and build phenomenal sales and revenue.

- Nike's "Just Do It"
- Apple's "Think Different"
- Dove's "Real Beauty"
- The ALS Ice Bucket Challenge

Nike's campaign helped ignite the brand and the phrase became part of the American lexicon.

When Steve Jobs returned to Apple, the intent was to demonstrate the company's renewed focus on creativity and position the firm as the leader in personal computers and technology. Apple's efforts would eventually create millions of evangelists for the brand who today own multiple Apple products from pcs to smartphones, to iPads, to watches.

"Real Beauty" is the centerpiece of a Dove campaign launched in 2004 and continuing today. The campaign promotes self-acceptance by featuring real women of diverse backgrounds. Revenues reportedly doubled within three years of the campaign launch. It has helped transform beauty standards and fostered body positivity among women worldwide.

The words "ice bucket" took on a whole new meaning in 2014. ALS created the Ice Bucket Challenge and it turned into a viral phenomenon. One of my favorite PR efforts, it was designed to help raise funds for Amyotrophic Lateral Sclerosis (ALS), a progressive neurodegenerative disease that affects nerve cells in the brain and spinal cord.

The Ice Bucket Challenge included participants filming themselves as a bucket of ice water was dumped over their heads. They would nominate others to do the same and encourage friends to donate to ALS. Videos of everyone's challenge would be taped and posted within 24 hours on social media. All types of celebrities joined in the fun including Tom Cruise, Mark Zuckerberg, Oprah Winfrey, Bill Gates, and even former President George W. Bush. The challenge helped raise over $115 million in the U.S. alone for ALS, compared with $2.8 million during the same period the year before.

The effort had the impact of a PR rocket ship, launching a communications outreach program into a movement.

More recently the release of the movie Barbie inspired a cultural phenomenon. Millions of the dolls' fans, young and old, dressed up in pink-like Barbie clothing and went to the theater to see the film. Hundreds of television stories and articles resulted worldwide.

The movie earned $1.5 billion.

Most businesses do not have the means or budget to create a global movement. But in the PR arena of strategic warfare with words, the right message can elevate your brand to the forefront, and like the ice bucket challenge, douse the competition.

TOOLBOX TAKEAWAYS

- ➢ Words have power, initiating or reducing conflicts, reducing tensions, or eliminating a hostile situation.
- ➢ Words build businesses, helping define a message that not only amplifies awareness but also sells products.
- ➢ Words add clarity to images, bringing depth and understanding and a call to action to photos and videos.

2
Rethink PR—It's Not Publicity

Yes, you read that correctly.

Many consider media coverage the holy grail of public relations. However, publicity in and of itself is *not* public relations.

The two are different.

Publicity is often defined as the attention or notice given to someone or something by the media. This can include:
- News coverage: TV stories and articles featured in print publications
- Digital stories: Separate coverage for publications you will only see online
- Social media: Photo and video placements geared to reach large audiences

Public Relations differs in that it is geared to an entire campaign effort to change behavior and reach a specific targeted outcome—whether with internal audiences (employees) or external audiences (customers, prospects and stakeholders).

Despite their distinct differences, the two often overlap in practice.

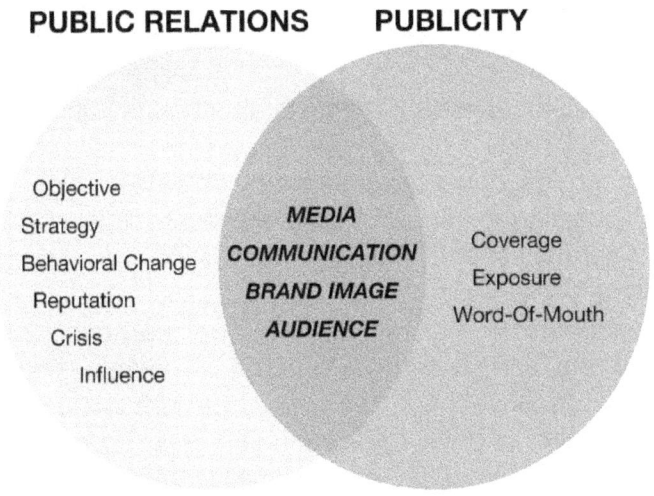

The PR campaign is planned, organized, analyzed, and agreed upon by upper management. It can include communication tools such as employee notices on the corporate web portal; an email newsletter to clients; articles, blogs, and videos on the company website; paid advertising, if necessary; and, as part of the communications plan, media relations.

Publicity is often sold as the end game, the whip cream on top of the sundae to help build a business and create some type of sustainability. Many books and articles entice the reader to believe they can gain national coverage and dramatically increase sales by following a few simple rules.

I chuckle when I see a book or article such as *"How to Get on the Today Show in Five Easy Steps"* or *"The Only Book You Will Need To Secure National Media Coverage."*

A few tips can be garnered through perusing one or more of these writings. However, media coverage, especially on a national basis, takes hours of planning and effort. Some top media professionals will discuss an article they secured in *The Wall Street Journal, New York Times,* or something similar. Some will discuss a recent client appearance on NBC News or Good Morning America.

They will impart how it took six months, perhaps a year, of endless effort to make it all happen.

While publicity creates interest and perhaps excitement for a short period of time, public relations focuses on the long game.

Think in terms of creating long lasting relationships with stakeholders both internally and externally. Think about establishing influence, trust and transparency. Consider perceptions, recruitment, behavioral change and long-term impact.

A company planning to open a new downtown high-rise hotel with an appealing restaurant will surely secure articles in the local media. They may even secure an interview or two on television or radio.

The accompanying press will focus on the project plans and may include a paragraph or two about ownership. The publicity certainly captures attention and generates buzz on social media.

While the media coverage is welcomed and valued, the entire public relations campaign should involve messaging strategies that go beyond the typical launch story.

One strategy could focus on the company itself. Community outreach methods to familiarize area leaders and influencers about hotel ownership and its track record of success of building similar structures in other communities. The goal is to build strong positive relationships and impact the community it serves.

Another strategy could focus on the owners themselves. Do the individuals have an interesting back story, something that could be leveraged for future articles and perhaps speaking engagements and/or board opportunities with local organizations?

A third strategy is recruitment. A large hotel and restaurant need people to run them. Ownership needs to create messaging to attract team members who wish to enhance their careers and are in-tune with the company's long-term objective. This can involve typical ads to interviews and postings on social media with current team members in other cities, to highlighting opportunities for personal growth on the company website and more.

Campaigns, like those mentioned earlier for Apple, Dove and Nike, take months of planning. It involves much more than trying to secure a few feature stories in the media.

In fact, not every campaign is centered on media coverage. Many campaigns involve outreach to specific groups such as women's organizations, business associations, or school boards where media relations may not be a factor.

Over time, I learned to be wary of any CEO or client who believes publicity for publicity's sake will help build their business.

I have known business owners who reveled in seeing their photo and name in a publication. They enjoyed getting pats on the back from friends and colleagues. Yet those efforts did little to define company messaging, raise awareness, or sell products. Eventually they curtailed the campaign saying the results were "mixed."

At the end of the day, an attempt to secure publicity with a lack of detailed messaging, planning, and strategy will fall on deaf ears with little return on investment.

TOOLBOX TAKEAWAYS

- Publicity in and of itself is not public relations.
- Public Relations is an overall strategic corporate effort to change behavior and reach a desired outcome.
- Publicity can be one part of a communications plan to reach targeted audiences.

3
Plan the Attack

No one wins a war by accident. A general would never go into battle without properly trained soldiers, necessary weaponry, strategic options, and a timeline to reach their objective. A complete plan to ensure victory.

Likewise, experienced PR professionals will tell you it's crucial to have a complete public relations plan in place before embarking on any type of campaign. Depending on the budget, the plan should involve research, programming, action steps, and, of course, evaluation.

Business owners can be their own worst enemy. I have heard more than one cry out for help promoting their company. Yet they think some media exposure will solve all their problems. They need exposure but are seeking a quick solution to increase branding and sales—instead of laying a foundation for success.

Some believe a few articles and interviews will enable them to rise above the competition.

Strategically, however, their conceived effort has little chance of succeeding. It not only leaves the business owner in trouble but also you, the PR professional.

Nearly all heads of organizations—whether they are publicly owned, privately held, or a non-profit—spend weeks and even months working on long-term plans and objectives for their business. They meet with the executive team, accountants, lawyers and others to determine what kind of staffing, dollars and resources it takes to achieve two-year, five-year, and even ten-year goals.

The same should be true for a public relations campaign. The campaign should include:

> **Research or Data Detailing a Current Problem or Need Within the Organization**

It can be as simple as overcoming a lack of product awareness or changing the perception of upper line management with remote team workers.

➤ **An Overall Campaign Goal**

This should be as specific as possible so it can be measured and evaluated.

The goal could range from educating the local community on the various programs available at a bank resulting in opening 100 new accounts within 12 months, to increasing a college's brand with high school students, resulting in a 20% increase in enrollments.

Time should be spent not only identifying the demographics of your audience-that is the likely users of your product (men 25-54, women 18-35 etc.) but also the psychographics of that audience whether they be business decision makers in a certain area, mothers of young children, income levels and more.

Detail each and every customer base you wish to reach or expand.

➤ **Specific Channels and Technologies to Best Reach Those Audiences**

This can include traditional media outreach (TV, newspaper, radio), customer lists, email lists, social media ads (Facebook, LinkedIn, TikTok, YouTube), social media optimization on search channels, hosting events, trade show booths/exhibits, charitable/community endeavors and more.

➤ **Measurement and Evaluation to Ensure the Right Type of Actions Are Taking Place**

Adjustments may be necessary to ensure the campaign remains on track for the desired outcomes. This can range from periodic customer surveys to an increase in web traffic to more signups or requests for specific products or services.

In some campaigns, special direct mailings, newsletters, webinars and speaking engagements may provide the desired result. Media relations may not be a part of the mix.

In an ideal world the PR pro or agency should be given the resources necessary to communicate with the business owner, sales managers, marketing personnel, downline staff and customers to get a real feel for what the actual PR goal should be. Then they can determine the messaging necessary to meet the objective.

Proper planning involves a symbiotic relationship between the CEO, marketing, and the PR agency or team. Time should be allocated to work through the strategies to ensure the success of any public relations campaign.

The right plan can help a business plant their flag atop the competitive hill.

As Sun Tzu, the great Chinese general and strategist, said "Every battle is won before it is fought."

TOOLBOX TAKEAWAYS

- Avoid the temptation to immediately jump into a media relations campaign despite the urgings of the CEO or client.
- Ensure the CEO is on-board with the budgeting for the time necessary to create an all-inclusive results-oriented campaign.
- Explore messaging options, clarify objectives, and gain final agreement and acceptance by upper management.

4
It's Not an Ad, It's PR

Nike: *Just Do It*
Coca-Cola: *Open Happiness*
McDonald's: *I'm Lovin' It*
Dunkin': *America Runs On Dunkin*

Companies invest millions of dollars crafting these powerful taglines—then pour tens of millions more into TV, radio, and social media advertising to embed these brand lines into the minds of consumers.

Public relations is different. Unlike advertising, there are no short slogans, no way to match dollars for dollars spent to products sold, and often, little control of final content.

Many business owners are well-schooled in advertising. They know how much to spend to generate a certain level of sales.

But, when it comes to PR, many are not familiar with the complexities or the benefits associated with a campaign. Some believe public relations is just another tool to sell more goods and services.

I've met business owners who think they are ready to create a budget for public relations. They have dedicated a large amount to advertising and are willing to provide a smaller amount to try "to do something" with PR.

On our blog site, PR At Work, we have written over 100 entries. One of our most popular blogs breaks down the difference between public relations and advertising. So, what sets public relations apart from advertising?

With public relations, the medium—newspaper, magazine, or social platform—controls the message.

With advertising, the client or business owner controls the message.

PUBLIC RELATIONS   ADVERTISING

Media Controls
Audience
Run Dates
Airtime
Messaging
Content
Editorial Direction

Client Controls
Audience
Investment
Messaging
Content
Medium
Run Dates

With advertising, businesses can decide when they want their ad to run, how big they want it, and what copy goes into the advertisement. In an ad campaign, you can target small publications or large ones. Then select one or more television stations, print publications, radio stations, or social outlets that best reach your desired audience. You can run billboards, Facebook and YouTube ads, Google search ads, or select from an entire host of advertising vehicles. You simply choose the one that best fits your objectives, your audience, and your budget.

There is no filter in advertising. Your audience gets your message directly—exactly the way you created it.

Public relations is different. You send news releases and pitch materials to editors and producers, hopeful of generating a story about your cause or business. An editor may wish to interview the CEO immediately—or file the information for a future article. They might include your material as part of a special section or a roundup of similar firms, where the business may be one of several discussed. Your CEO may end up with only a small quote, among many others.

You have no control if an editor will run your news item, when they will run it, or how it will be used.

In some cases, an editor may even choose to skip the same key points you outlined in your pitch. They may take the story in an entirely different direction. Your pitch might include the necessary highlights: new expansion, largest facility in the region, new product line, new customer focus, why now, CEO's prospects for growth and expansion, and value to the community.

Yet the final version may only include one or more of the desired messaging strategies.

The story could even highlight a competitive company. An accompanying photo might feature a business different than yours.

The ability to craft a successful PR campaign is an entirely different skill set than those used in advertising.

Experienced public relations practitioners understand the nuances between publicity and advertising. They realize the final message may differ from its original intent when an article is published.

Understanding the differences between advertising and public relations can help you determine separate messaging strategies. It can improve the results of both your advertising efforts and your PR campaign.

TOOLBOX TAKEAWAYS

- Paid advertising provides message control.
- PR cedes final control to media.
- PR messaging strategies require a different expertise than advertising.

5
PR Is More Effective Than Advertising

Red Bull Stratos: *The Free Fall from Space*
Dove Real Beauty: *Body Positivity*
The Stanley Quencher: *Tumbler and Hydration Style*

These PR campaigns turned into their own movements. They generated great brand awareness not because of advertising but because of public relations efforts, spawning millions of dollars of earned media on television, social media and in print.

In fact, depending on the objective, a well-conceived public relations campaign will consistently outperform any straight ad spend. Usually for a fraction of the investment.

A recent study from 2014 by Nielsen, commissioned by inPowered, focused on the role of content in the consumer decision-making process. It concluded that PR is almost 90% more effective than advertising.

Even if those numbers are slightly inflated, studies have shown news stories have at least a 3 to 1 advantage in memorability rate when compared to advertising.

Think about it.

When was the last time you went to a news site to look at advertisements?

How many times have you whisked past those annoying pop-up ads on social media, preventing you from reading an interesting post or article?

Consumers wish to be educated and entertained. They consume newspaper and magazine articles, TV news programs, radio interviews, podcast interviews, YouTube videos, and more to stay informed and make better decisions.

Media communications, when done effectively, can help motivate a buyer to purchase a product or service or take some kind of action—going well beyond the scope of a series of advertisements.

Many of these efforts are highlighted in the campaigns section of this book. I've seen firsthand when campaigns delivered outstanding results for the client—with little to no ad spend.

- Radio interviews helped spike seminar ticket sales.
- Articles have boosted traffic and sales at a classic car dealership.
- Podcasts have ignited book sales.
- Feature articles helped an architectural firm gain major contracts.
- National press built relationships and new business for a commercial woodworking company.

A targeted media relations campaign provides a wide range of benefits for any business or organization.

The major benefit is credibility.

An article or TV feature highlighting a company serves as a third-party endorsement for the business. It goes beyond an organization saying "we're great, do business with us" to one where the media is touting a firm as an outstanding company, essentially telling readers to do business with them.

Reputation enhancement is another benefit.

A news story can spotlight a company's involvement with charitable and civic organizations. It can demonstrate how the business has an interest in not only sales and profits, but also as a trusted member of the community it serves. It can showcase the firm in an entirely new light, eliciting favorable feedback from readers and viewers.

On a larger scale, Lowe's has their own community revitalization program called *Lowe's Hometowns*. As of this writing, Lowe's is awarding $10 million in grants to fund 100 renovations and complete an additional 1,700 improvement projects. A compelling twist—the projects are selected by Lowe's associates. This not only empowers the employees to have a voice in how the company gives back to the community, but it builds internal trust and strengthens community ties. Lowe's is promoting the initiative and generating valuable earned media in the process.

Many locally based businesses are also quick to lend a hand when their communities need them most. From restaurants and banks to retailers, they rally teams to support neighborhoods impacted by disasters such as fires or tornados. These efforts build cohesion and strengthen the organization from within. Photos and videos appear on social media, prompting supportive messages from friends, neighbors, and colleagues—reinforcing both team morale and community connection.

Red Bull, Dove, Stanley, and Lowe's are examples of companies that invested not only in a campaign, but in the betterment of their communities. Businesses and organizations, both large and small, can follow their lead by developing a public relations plan that creates real, lasting impact in their community.

Plans that not only enhance brand and reputation, but also deliver benefits that far exceed those generated by typical advertising.

TOOLBOX TAKEAWAYS

- PR has benefits more effective than advertising.
- PR adds credibility and enhances reputation.
- PR helps build positive impact within the local community.

6
Building an Objective to Drive Results

The ALS Ice Bucket Challenge is a great example of a PR campaign that succeeded on many levels.

Why? It all began with a tangible objective.

In the case of ALS, the goal was clear—build the brand and raise funding. While no one foresaw the campaign becoming a cultural phenomenon that would eventually raise $220 million, the goal was clear and documented.

Public Relations campaigns work best when a well thought out objective is established.

It should be as tangible as possible.

Increasing branding and awareness with potential customers is surely a desired output of any PR campaign, but that alone can be hard to measure.

Thousands of dollars in time or fees can be spent generating a series of articles about a company. Yet without a documented goal, a CEO may not realize any impact from the campaign. They may pull the plug and terminate the effort.

Instead, focus on a number or action you want to achieve with objectives that can be developed and measured.

"Build relationships with key target audiences to help sell 1000 custom-made wooden toy trucks in 12 months."

"Generate 100,000 signatures to add a special proposition on the next ballot."

In the first example, the business can easily measure whether it is selling any toy trucks. Through a series of strategies working hand-in-hand with the sales and fulfillment team, the business could embark on a number of tactics:

- Developing proper messaging about the trucks
- Distinguishing their toy trucks from others in the marketplace
- Generating articles in targeted general interest, toy, and child-oriented publications
- Creating or enhancing their newsletter
- Altering or adding to their website
- Showcasing trucks on YouTube videos, Facebook, TikTok and other platforms
- Inviting TV news crews to create stories on the manufacturing of the trucks
- Hosting special events to bring families to the facility to "test drive" the trucks

In six months, the sales team should have sold around 500 trucks with several pending orders in the pipeline. If interest lags, the company can adjust their approach. It can refine its sales message and communications strategy. Perhaps the company might even need to change the audience profile it thought would be most interested in this product.

It might also have to change the product itself to better meet customer needs.

In the second example, a political campaign can focus on educating area residents about the benefits of adding a special amendment to the ballot. The goal is to gather enough signatures to bring the issue to a public vote. The tactics can include:

- Petition signing events at local shops or grocers
- Direct mailers to area residents
- Issue discussion at town hall meetings
- Engaging in TV and radio interviews
- Writing op-eds in local newspapers
- Running organic and paid social media campaigns
- Placing ads in print/digital publications

Periodic check-ins can measure if the numbers are in-line with the eventual target date.

If people are hesitant to sign the petition you can adjust and perhaps even change the wording of the amendment to help residents better understand the issue. The amendment campaign is very measurable.

When the deadline arrives, you either have 100,000 signatures or you don't.

Business owners and others seeking a solid return on investment from their PR campaign should ensure they create objectives that can be measured. Similar to the Ice Bucket Challenge, the goal should be not just to generate articles—it's to change the audience's behavior and deliver real results.

It may even turn a grassroots effort into a global movement.

TOOLBOX TAKEAWAYS

- ➢ PR works best with a tangible objective.
- ➢ Campaign results should be measurable.
- ➢ Adjust campaigns as necessary for best results.

7
Media Relations: The Inside Pitch

The inside pitch of media relations isn't just about getting the hits—it's about timing, strategy, and creating the message to shift the game in your favor.
Think of it as an art.

It begins with building relationships with journalists, writers and influencers. Not just to land a one-off feature, but to support them in developing and broadcasting a story that delivers high value to their audience.

It is a process that demonstrates your expertise in the subject matter and your ability to make it all happen quickly, from start to finish. This is what separates true professionals from the inexperienced practitioner.

Media relations specialists are held in high esteem by reporters who continue to contact them for additional stories and input. It is a relationship that can last years, even decades. The end result helps you and your business build its brand, boost visibility, and earn the public's trust.

PR planning helps brands develop their message and identify target audiences. Media relations comes into play when you need to reach external audiences, customers, and prospects—those who can benefit from your products and services.

It's when you want to cast a wider net and expand your reach.

Think in terms of Apple launching a new iPhone, McDonald's introducing a new sandwich, or GM rolling out a new vehicle. These brands generate millions of dollars in earned media—through consumer publications, trade journals, TV news stories, and on social media. This happens long before launching any related advertising. The same holds true for smaller companies whose audiences are more localized or niche oriented.

As highlighted in Section II (Campaigns) of this book, Cohen Woodworking leveraged a major award it received and built a successful media relations campaign—generating tens of thousands of dollars in earned media. Author Paul Bruno utilizes media relations to promote his books on early Jeep history, and Daniel Schmitt & Co. Classic Cars focuses on enticing stories to generate local showroom traffic and sell cars globally.

A public relations campaign can cover many different channels to improve brand awareness. More channels give your brand and customers a better chance to connect. PR professionals use channels including:

- Social media
- Influencer endorsements
- Traditional media
- Press releases
- Public events
- Owned media-blogs, corporate photos, and videos

Media relations, however, only uses one channel—the press, which today includes not only TV, radio, and print vehicles but also podcasts and social channels. Specialists contact journalists and writers to spread the business's story across print and broadcast platforms.

In many cases, media relations can be applied as an educational vehicle to help the community understand and support a political endeavor or related initiative. Like any effective vehicle, the message needs direction and fuel—strategic messaging, timely interviews, and well-placed op-eds. By partnering with trusted media, PR professionals can guide public understanding and rally community support around a cause or ballot measure.

At the same time, media relations supports and boosts visibility at the organizational level.

We are often contacted by a journalist or editor to interview the CEO of one of our client companies, with urgent requests for a photo, video, or key talking points. The PR professional should know how to quickly reach the CEO or point person, and have access to key resources like headshots, bios, and video clips. These resources should be organized and ready to be delivered at a moment's notice.

Consistently delivering key information in a timely manner establishes you and your client as a trusted resource. You become "top-of-mind" when a journalist seeks insight on a current business trend or needs to do an interview after a cancellation—which has happened on more than one occasion.

A solid relationship also helps pique a producer's interest and receptivity when your business has news to disseminate. It yields not just one story but perhaps 5, 10, or more.

Over the years I have developed bonds with many journalists. One such example was a collaboration with a writer for a local business publication. Together, we secured many feature stories spotlighting our clients. At one point, the publication's photographer remarked, "My goodness, it seems most of the writer's features center on Solomon Turner clients!"

We get our share—and then some.

Publicity vs. Media Relations

Many believe publicity and media relations are the same. While they intersect—the two are different. Some associate publicity with the idea of generating as much media coverage as possible without necessarily having a long-range plan or objective. In the industry, this is called the "spray and pray" method of PR. Distribute as many news releases as possible to as many journalists as possible, and hope you get a large number of "hits." This may work in the short term, but fails to build relationships with journalists in the long term.

It may not even yield high-quality content or highlight the intended message.

The volume of articles, TV stories, blogs, and digital placements should not determine the success or failure of the PR effort. Without a clear, defined goal—with little intent on building long-term relationships—these one-and-done efforts often yield little fruit and fail to move the needle. We will explore various methods to generate successful media coverage in later chapters.

While PR and media relations are two separate functions, specialists in each area can work together to create the right type of media outreach that attracts your buyer. Together, it gives you a way to share news while attracting targeted producers and writers. In the end, you'll improve your campaign's reach while gaining the right kind of message dissemination and better outcomes.

The result?

An inside pitch that lands on the barrel of the PR bat and turns a few singles into a bevy of homeruns.

TOOLBOX TAKEAWAYS

- Media Relations and Public Relations are two different functions.
- Media Relations improves messaging and reach with external audiences.
- Media Relations specialists help build relationships with targeted journalists resulting in not just one but multiple stories.

8
Media Relations: The Strategy

"The medium is the message."
-- Marshall McLuhan

McLuhan, a Canadian philosopher and media theorist, coined this phrase to emphasize that the medium shapes how a message is understood—often more than the content itself. Different media engages different human senses, which influences how the message is processed and experienced.

Selecting the right medium or media is important in choosing the right channel that speaks to your audience. It is the focus of any media relations strategy. Any type of media campaign planning should begin with analysis of the needs of the client and their goals.

- **Short-term:** Event, new product, or book launch
- **Mid-range:** Thought leadership
- **Long-term:** Ongoing brand building, multiple product launches, community relations

The next step is to determine the entire scope of the campaign. Is it global, national or local? Will the focus involve trade or consumer outlets—or both? Are there enticing visual elements to grab the attention of an editor, reporter, and producer, important in today's visually based media terrain?

Once the campaign length and scope are determined then the proper medium or media can be selected. A listing of the tools needed for each medium should then be detailed and gathered. This can include key research-based data, photos, videos, whitepapers, news releases and short interviews with CEOs and/or principals (both in video and print format). Each may have different technical requirements which will need to be addressed.

Media Channels

Choosing the right media channel is key to how a message is not only delivered but received. These can span both traditional and digital formats—from television and print to podcasts and online publications.

Television

Television requires strong visual components to coincide with any interview. In many cases, shooting will focus not only on a product but how the product is made. In some cases, company supplied video or B Roll can be prepared and delivered to the reporter to complete their piece.

Reporters may wish to interview the CEO as well as other team members. New product users could also be part of the interview focus. Depending on need and timeliness, some interviews may be conducted via Zoom or other online vehicle. For virtual interviews, the interviewee should have a comfortable and professional space with an appropriate background.

Newspaper

Newspaper reporters are interested in consumer or business trends and how your story fits into that landscape. Any research or data is helpful when stating your case for coverage.

The business owner or interviewee should be well-schooled in all aspects of the highlighted product and process—and able to communicate those details clearly. Should the reporter want to conduct an in-depth interview, the subject should be prepared for a lengthy Q&A session.

Additionally, photographs will be needed to supplement the narrative of the story. The business should be prepared for a photo shoot that can involve multiple aspects of a company's operation.

Business & Trade Journals

Trade articles focus on a particular industry with regard to business trends, past successes and the future trajectory of a featured company.

These reporters will need more hard data about the business than those required by a newspaper journalist.

An interview will be required to cover all aspects of the company's operation. Photos will be needed to highlight the story.

Radio

Depending upon the subject matter, a radio interview can last anywhere from five minutes to much longer. Most interviews focus on a community event, an exciting new product launch, or a business making a positive impact on a local community.

The interviewee should be well prepped to discuss their subject in depth. Voice inflection and interesting stories are necessary to engage the host and the audience.

For best results the interview should be conducted in-person at the station's studio. The guest is then able to build camaraderie with the interviewer and could potentially be given a longer interview—or even asked to return for a second appearance. The sound quality is also superior to that completed remotely over the phone.

Podcasts

Podcast interviews are generally long and in-depth sessions. They can range from 30 minutes to well over one hour. In most cases they are conducted over Zoom or a similar video platform. Many podcasts are aired not only on audio channels, but also on YouTube.

Interviewees should be prepared for a lengthy session and have the appropriate equipment to ensure a high-quality audio and on-camera appearance. The right type of background should be created in-line with the desired image and brand. Additional lighting may be needed.

Subjects should dress appropriately and should be prepared to be entertaining as well as insightful.

Press Releases

Press releases are a necessity for public companies and others wishing to convey their latest quarterly results to the media and stakeholders. Smaller businesses can use them to provide depth and detail to any email pitch. Many sites will also publish a press release at little to no charge, helping build brand and search engine optimization.

Magazines

Magazine articles provide long, in-depth accounts of newsmakers and other personalities. The focus is on content that will be of importance outside the 24-hour news cycle. These features usually have long lead times and are accompanied by photos and graphics. They can appear in both print and digital versions. They are a good resource for celebrities and thought leaders wishing to publicize a book or movie as they enhance their personal brand.

Online Publications

In the growing digital ecosystem, many publishers have forsaken all printed materials and shifted focus to purely online products. Depending on the publication the articles tend to be longer form with accompanying photos and even links to videos and websites. Like magazines they are a good source to build brand for companies and individuals.

Social Media

Social media can serve as its own group of mediums-think Facebook, Instagram, LinkedIn, TikTok, and X-with ads, videos and short postings. Many use this as a tool to reach young consumers. Others employ it to amplify article placements in newspapers, and TV interviews. Any placement can be linked and given additional exposure on social channels.

No matter the medium, the key to delivering impact is to tailor your approach. Success lies in understanding the strengths of each channel and using them to amplify your message.

Similar to the entire public relations campaign, the media relations effort also demands in-depth planning. The goal is to be prepared to deliver short and insightful answers, be ready for any curveballs that may be thrown their way, and ensure the message is delivered and received by the audience in an impactful manner.

Regardless of any dispute over McLuhan's claim that the medium is the message, these facts remain—pairing the right media with the right audience and the right approach is the cornerstone of a successful campaign. Mastering the balance between the message and the right medium moves the needle from merely informing the audience to taking compelling action.

TOOLBOX TAKEAWAYS

- Selecting the medium that best reaches the desired audience is crucial to campaign success.
- The necessary tools should be created and available to help each journalist develop their story.
- Media training may be necessary to help the interviewee optimize any TV or print interview.

9
PR Pros Aren't Liars

Wait...what?

Andrew Cohen, a lawyer turned communications expert, once delivered a scathing critique of the PR industry on *CBS Sunday Morning*. Commenting on a memoir by former White House press secretary Scott McClellan—who admitted to manipulating facts to justify the Iraq War—Cohen said, "Show me a PR person who is accurate and truthful, and I'll show you a PR person who is unemployed." Cohen further stated that PR pros are hired because they are trained for their ability to spin half-truths or to be untruthful.

Cohen's comments resonated throughout the profession.

The Public Relations Society of America (PRSA) developed a long-standing code of ethics as a guide for practicing PR professionals. Those ethics focus on advocacy, honesty, expertise, independence (accountability), loyalty and fairness.

Cohen compared the Code to "The Burglars Association of America [having] as its creed 'Thou Shalt Not Steal."

I consider myself a PR professional who is employed. So, does that make me a liar?

Cohen would still think so.

Public relations professionals are trained and highly skilled in message creation and delivery. They are not—as some say—spin doctors, propagandists, or spinmeisters. They don't believe in the old saying any publicity is good publicity as long as they spell my name right.

While many associate PR with publicists for glamorous Hollywood stars and candidates for political office, most public relations pros work behind the scenes to connect a business or organization with the community they serve.

In many cases, they establish platforms not only for audience connection, but also shared experiences, helping stakeholders foster a sense of ownership and collective action. In times of crisis, they can help a community restore hope and morale by sharing positive narratives and stories of resilience.

Consider an organization like Habitat for Humanity—they leverage PR to promote their work, mobilizing volunteers and donors to provide housing for deserving families.

Projects like The Underline in Miami utilize PR to build support from the community, government, and private sectors for transformative urban revitalization.

TOMS shoes is among the many corporations that have built their brand around sustainability, transparency, and giving—donating over 100 million shoes to children worldwide since the start of their campaign in 2006.

Over the years, I have met dozens, if not hundreds, of employed public relations professionals. While none were press secretaries to a president or the chief spokesperson for a Fortune 10 company, most are hardworking individuals steadily building successful careers.

Nearly all serve as the voice of their clients, communicating key messages to the public and stakeholders through the media. They form mutually beneficial relationships with journalists, helping them with ideas and information to do their jobs more efficiently.

When necessary, they take the glass half-full approach as opposed to half-empty.

But they do not create misleading information or knowingly overly state earnings—just to get a story.

Cohen verbally pillaged an entire industry because one person didn't have the courage to step away from something he did not believe in. Cohen himself was creating misinformation.

And it was deceitful.

TOOLBOX TAKEAWAYS

- Focus on accuracy and truthfulness.
- In times of crisis defend, deflect, and delay if necessary but do not create misinformation.
- Establish a personal ethical line, and if asked, refuse to cross it.

10
The PR Big Top: Juggling Negativity

P.T. Barnum, the legendary showman of Barnum & Bailey Circus, was once asked about negative stories in the newspaper commenting:
> "*I don't care what the newspapers say about me as long as they spell my name right.*"

In the late 19th century, unfavorable press may not have harmed Barnum—but today's media landscape is an entirely different circus. The ringmasters have expanded from newspaper, television and radio to social channels like Facebook, Instagram, TikTok and X.

In today's fast-moving arena, negative business news spreads quickly and gains traction in hours.

And it can have a major impact.

How does it happen? An employee discovers unfavorable news. They discuss it with a teammate. Soon they post on Facebook, TikTok, or X.

Depending on the authenticity and severity of the news, those posts can get noticed by reporters at local TV stations and newspapers. Quickly they become stories in the mass media.

They get recorded and photographed. Edited and enhanced. Reconstructed and retold.

Then it surfaces—not on just one or two, but dozens of social and digital platforms. The audience grows from a few to hundreds of thousands.

Most large corporations and even smaller firms will at some point face a situation that can lead to negative coverage. Major catastrophic events such as a fire, on-site hostage situation, or a weather-related building collapse may be rare. But they are incidents that send shocks through the community.

Depending on the life-threatening nature of the incident, local TV news vans will ascend quickly. National media may also appear. The business has little time to react.

Media attention can focus on other types of incidents such as an online data breach, a ransom request, a new major lawsuit against the business, or a large downsizing of employees.

Amidst the chaos—any messaging or situational control can quickly get lost.

Perhaps the worst disaster, marked by a notably slow response, was the BP Oil Spill in 2010. Many call it the worst large-scale environmental disaster in world history.

The Deepwater Horizon was drilling for oil on behalf of BP about 40 miles off the Louisiana coast. It exploded and a fire raged. Eleven were killed and 17 were injured. The blowout sank the drilling unit and caused a massive oil spill in the Gulf of Mexico.

Millions of gallons of oil were spilled. Extensive damage occurred to marine and wildlife habitats as well as fishing and tourism industries. Dolphins and other wildlife are said to have died in record numbers. Oil was found not only in Louisiana, but also in the Florida Panhandle and Tampa Bay.

Many facets of the disaster, including clean-up and recovery, were featured nightly on network news broadcasts. They received ongoing coverage on 24-hour news channels.

BP was slow and stoic in its response.

There was no admonition of guilt. The company's CEO at the time, Tony Howard, eventually made an appearance in Louisiana and walked the coastline. When asked about the incident he said, "I just want my life back." This drew the ire of hundreds of fishermen and others whose livelihood was crushed by the incident.

Howard would later apologize for his remarks—but the damage was done.

BP had difficulties capping the oil leak. It continued for years. The company was fined tens of billions of dollars and its reputation damaged. I still think about those events every time I pass a BP convenience station.

While a business cannot control all aspects of an incident, it can take necessary steps to avoid a free-for-all with the media. Here are a few strategies to limit, or reduce, the impact of negative news when it appears to be coming your way:

1. Be Prepared.

First, have a crisis communications plan in place. You never know what can happen in the day-to-day operation of even a small business. Work with your PR team or agency and identify risks. Develop responses. A business owner should be prepared for a fire, disgruntled customers, an employee that gets too aggressive with customers or becomes unstable, food poisoning (restaurants or supermarkets), or even a security breach.

2. Determine the Severity of the Negative News.

Did you get a small negative mention in the newspaper or something that can be misconstrued as negative? Is there one angry customer who is ticked off about an item? Or did a TV station do a virtual "hammer job" on your business where 12 angry customers were on camera all complaining about your bad service, a troublesome employee, or defective merchandise? The severity of the negative press will determine what steps to take next.

3. In Most Cases, the Best Course of Action is No Action.

If the incident was relatively minor, then the best course of action would be to let it pass. In the 24-hour news cycle, most people will glance over anything that isn't a major story or something that doesn't get published in multiple outlets. In most cases, there's no need to fan the flames and make the situation worse than it is. If the negative press is a very minor mention in a newspaper, and not really an issue or a problem, there is no need to run ads apologizing for any mishaps. Drawing more attention to the issue only pours gasoline on the fire.

4. Take a Proactive Approach When the Issue Becomes Serious.

Get out in front of any serious issue that could negatively impact the company. If you learn in advance from a customer or contact that a newspaper or TV station is going to do a negative story—don't hide from it. Failing to respond to multiple media requests implies your firm is "guilty" of some violation, whether true or not. Instead, take precautions to fix the issue. Companies can be proactive by issuing a letter to the media or to customers. This is a typical corporate response that is usually effective:

> "We realize that there was an issue with our delivery system, and sincerely apologize for any inconvenience this may have caused our customers. We have made staff changes and implemented system improvements to prevent this from happening in the future. Customers should no longer experience any issues. In the meantime, we are happy to honor merchandise returns or cash reimbursements if needed. If you encounter any issues, please call or text us. Thank you for your understanding and continued support, we look forward to continuing to serve your needs."

5. Take Caution About Granting Interviews.

If a situation is spiraling out of control, the owner may feel compelled to appear on camera or answer tough questions with a newspaper reporter. They should first secure some media training. The owner should be schooled and prepared to answer probing inquiries. Physical appearance plays a strong role in how the public perceives the owner, the company, and the situation. This includes wearing the proper attire and hosting the interview in the proper setting. Take a proactive approach and avoid the "gotcha" parking lot camera crews.

6. Watch and Learn.

Read the newspaper and digital publications, watch TV news, both network and local, and monitor any social channels. Keep an eye out for any stories that could be a crisis or a negative situation. Watch how those firms or organizations react. Some schools and major companies have a good plan to handle negative press. Some do not. It becomes obvious when a major chain or business keeps getting blasted by the type of response.

A business owner needs to be prepared for anything that could go wrong. They need to have a plan in place for any type of crisis or negative situation. At the same time, they need to be astute enough to analyze if some negative news is really "negative" and how it will impact their business. Is the situation damaging? If the answer is "no" then don't spend time making the problem worse. If the answer is "yes" then take the appropriate action to first fix the problem and then let the appropriate media know the problem is resolved.

The goal is to avoid an all-out media circus. Don't be Tony Howard. Be prepared.

TOOLBOX TAKEAWAYS

- Be prepared, create a crisis communications plan, and have it available in case of emergency.
- Don't overreact, analyze and determine if a small negative article is worthy of a response.
- When a response is necessary, take responsibility and communicate sincerely and transparently. Detail action steps taken to prevent a reoccurrence.

11
Strike Zone: Managing the Media

Three strikes and you're out!

You don't have to be a baseball fan to know the strike zone is key—pitch outside it, you lose control; pitch inside it, you have a shot at striking out the batter. Navigating the media during a campaign works much the same way. If you target the right audience with the right message, you've thrown a great pitch. Miss, and you're off the mark. To deliver the message successfully, you must understand the dynamics of working with the media.

Managing the Message—and the Game

How a company manages the media will make or break any type of strategically developed communications plan. CEOs or business leaders may speak to reporters annually, others quarterly, while many seem to always have a video camera in sight.

Few need to communicate with the media more than Major League Baseball managers.

It is a key part of their skill set. How they interact with reporters can help make or break a team's performance, impact individual players, motivate a fan base, and propel the future of an entire organization.

Additionally, these confabs help managers build or enhance their own reputation and build confidence with their stakeholders that they will get the job done.

These baseball leaders provide lessons for those who interact with TV, social media, and print media. They can be studied and practiced. Business executives can learn much about tone setting, word selection, and shaping the narrative. The best of which can be applied for anyone's communications toolbox.

Like most CEOs, managers are hired based on their strong tactical skills and leadership abilities. They must guide a team through a long 162-game regular season, and hopefully a playoff run. They deal with individual players, make lineups, manage a team through a game they hope to win, and laud and cajole players afterwards.

As part of their job, they must also become masters of the media.

Managers spend a large part of their game day speaking with newspaper, TV, radio and online reporters. Much more than fans realize.

Early in my career, I was a sports reporter and broadcaster and witnessed this firsthand. As the team warms up before game time, a manager will sit in the dugout and reporters will gather. Initial social conversation changes to questions dealing with that night's lineup, updates on injured players, or insights on up-and-coming minor leaguers.

The manager and the media know what to expect. Still, cognizant of the scrutiny of social media the manager must choose his words carefully. He doesn't want to convey anything that could be misconstrued by his own players, opponent, or umpire—and turned into a viral circus.

After the game, the manager again meets with reporters. This time the gathering is more formal and resembles a news conference. Reporters representing all the area's major media players are represented. Much of it is aired live on the channel or network that carried the game broadcast.

Players watch, absorb and reflect the tone of their manager. Many managers use these post-game events as a bully pulpit to communicate with the team.

Baseball managers use their pulpit to not only inspire their team but, in a winning scenario, the fans as well. They spend six months conversing with all types of reporters and do so each day, every day.

The best ones know how to expertly relate to the media.

The same holds for corporate executives, thought leaders, and field experts. Those who stand out are featured regularly on news networks. They are highly skilled communicators. These individuals stay on-point, reflect corporate or brand messaging and convey confidence. They portray an image reflective and perhaps enhancing their perceived business or personal brand value.

The Power of the Written Word

Whitey Herzog managed the St. Louis Cardinals baseball team in the 1980s, leading them to three pennants and a World Championship. A Hall-of-Fame manager, Herzog was an outstanding communicator, winning the confidence of upper management, and was revered by the fans. I sat in on many interviews with the late Whitey Herzog during the time he managed the St. Louis Cardinals.

He realized early on that his strongest allies would be the reporters behind the printed word.

Herzog spent a lot of time with newspaper writers and, to the delight of those in the print media, cast aside any TV or radio journalist that happened to walk into his office seeking an interview.

During the playoffs in the mid-1980s I saw a camera crew waltz into Herzog's office. I laughed anticipating the result. Sure enough, a few seconds later they were sent on their way.

Herzog figured he could never upset anyone or get fired for anything he said on radio or television. But he realized the newspaper was a different story (pardon the pun).

While that approach served Herzog well in the 1980s, it would amount to a large PR crisis today, where any inflammatory verbal exchange with a reporter of any ilk would be recorded and played multiple times on social channels. It would result in a large problem, not only for the manager, but team ownership as well.

Still the lesson here is that forming positive relationships with key journalists can help advance the brand, mission, and cause of any organization.

Leveraging the Media

Tony LaRussa served as the manager of the St. Louis Cardinals, leading the team to several National League pennants and two World Series Championships. Though I didn't get to witness any of his press conferences in person, LaRussa also knew how to use the media to his advantage. In St. Louis his post-game media sessions were among the first to air live.

LaRussa didn't mind discussing his in-game decision making but could get verbally combative if he didn't like a reporter's question.

His responses could often be argumentative if not unpredictable.

Fans enjoyed watching him chastise a reporter or challenge a writer to further explain his question. In many households it became must-see TV. His success on the field enabled him to avoid negativity associated with managers of losing teams.

While LaRussa certainly gained attention for his unpredictable interviews, it does demonstrate the risk of losing control over the message on live television. High-pressure moments and unfiltered reactions can shape public perception and dominate the headlines—and not always in the best light. Off the field, the PR professional must help the client learn to master composure, control the narrative, and manage the tone of the interview, despite any challenging interactions.

Winning the Game

Similar to their baseball brethren, managing perceptions and bolstering team performance are key for business leaders. By tapping into their communications toolbox—interviews, podcasts, social media, newspapers, and television—they can shape the narrative and drive home a winning campaign.

Like the well-timed call to the bullpen, the right tool at the right moment can make all the difference. CEOs can recognize highly achieving employees in a regular corporate communique. They can discuss new areas of customer focus, new products, and new long-term plans in a company town hall.

Key messaging can be carried into articles and interviews that reflect the business's upward trajectory. Positive articles on a company can enhance reputation, differentiate the business from the competition, boost the team (employees), and fan base (customers).

A CEO or business owner may not be able to win a World Series, but they should aspire to win the game of media relations.

TOOLBOX TAKEAWAYS

- Business leaders can learn from baseball managers on how they utilize media relations to their advantage.
- The proper communications approach can motivate the team, fans (customers) and the entire organization.
- The end result is reputation enhancement, business differentiation, and potentially increased revenue.

12
Swimming with PR Sharks

The PR pool is infested with sharks.

Those who are constantly in motion, swimming about furiously to land the next big client or top-tier media placement.

Succeed and they live on in search of their next prey. Fail—and they'll retreat to the deep blue sea, searching for other less satisfying opportunities.

Much like sharks strategically moving from one fish-laden pod to the next, to survive, PR professionals need to constantly refine their approach. In the ocean of public relations, this includes recrafting the pitch and resorting to good old-fashioned storytelling. Whether it's pursuing a new client or a top journalist, public relations professionals are always selling.

The best story usually wins.

Many traits common to public relations are displayed weekly on a television show called *Shark Tank*. The reality program launched in 2009 on ABC and continues as of this writing.

Shark Tank focuses on aspiring entrepreneurs who seek to secure investments and partnerships with one or more of the "Sharks"—billionaires and millionaires who seek to grow their fortunes by investing in companies with high growth potential.

The ambitious, small business owner who gains an appearance in front of the investors is similar to an agency executive. They must develop a coherent presentation, quickly state their case, and pique the interest of a shark or two. That pitch must be well organized and on-point with a growing industry trend or consumer need—based on numbers that project a trajectory of high growth.

As one who has done a fair amount of pitching, it's not difficult to watch and ascertain who has the best chance of closing a deal. Many are infested with mistakes, preventing the striving business from getting an investment on *Shark Tank* and, for that matter, anywhere else.

The program provides many lessons for PR pros wishing to refine their pitching skills:

Construct a Clear, Concise Business Presentation

Many of the *Shark Tank* contestants seek to be creative. Some downright funny. Others are extremely nervous, barely able to get the words out of their mouth.

No matter how entertaining, those who appear disorganized and unable to state their case are usually sent home without funding.

In many ways the same holds true for PR pros seeking to build relationships at networking events, trade shows, and meetings with potential clients. Some lack the approach or the skills necessary to get a prospective buyer to the "tell me more" stage of the presentation.

Instead, focus on the core message and the audience you serve.

Strengthen and align your pitch with the client's needs, challenges, and expectations. Consider the following examples:

> "We just helped a help a business like yours increase their branding and awareness, and positively impact their sales team with a 30% increase in revenue. Would you like to hear how we did it?"

> "Have you heard of the now famous Acme Company? Our team just put together a media relations campaign that resulted in articles in The Wall Street Journal, New York Times, Forbes, USA Today, and appearances on FOX News, CNN, and more. Working in conjunction with your marketing, I believe we can do the same for you. Would you like to hear more?"

Know Your Numbers

On *Shark Tank*, entrepreneurs must know their revenue figures and be able to communicate them to the Sharks. This includes specific numbers for the last three years, last year—even last month.

Beyond the numbers, they must identify if sales are increasing or decreasing, and if any major orders are pending. Perhaps there is a logical explanation of how the company will grow over time.

Lack of hard numbers will usually send the entrepreneur packing.

In the case of a PR pitch, those "numbers" should include some understanding of the potential client's industry and where they stand among their competitors. They should include some case studies of working with similar companies and how your agency is a good fit for the client's needs. Finally, they should demonstrate that your agency is in a growth stage, with the team and expertise to help that client achieve their communications objective.

Know the Competition

As *Shark Tank's* "Mr. Wonderful," Kevin O' Leary often says, "Why should I invest in you when a multi-billion-dollar corporation can make the same thing and squash you like a cockroach?"

Business owners should study their competition and ensure their product or service provides them with a competitive advantage—something difficult to duplicate.

The same is true for agencies who need to demonstrate their expertise in a particular niche or product segment. On *Shark Tank*, companies lacking differentiation are usually shown the door. The same holds true for PR firms looking to gain share against older, more established competitors.

Understand Customer Acquisition

A recurring Shark's question is, "How much does it cost for you to acquire a customer?" Some entrepreneurs know the number, some do not.

The figure, of course, varies depending on the type of customer (business or consumer) and length of the selling cycle.

Those with unintelligible or extremely high numbers are asked to find another pool to swim in.

A PR firm owner should study their own cost of acquisition number. Adjustments can be made to assure profitability targets and maintain competitive advantage.

Time and costs of pitching vs. results.

Highlight Strengths; Hide Weaknesses

Potential "investees" often get hung up when a shark brings up a negative but minor point. The entrepreneur can get flustered. Even argumentative.

Suddenly a non-issue becomes a major concern.

The discussion shifts quickly away from the product and

focuses on the credibility of the individual. Fearing a personality clash, the sharks shy away. What appeared to be a good investment a minute ago suddenly gets water-logged.

Should a PR pitch turn negative, shift the focus to all the problem-solving aspects your agency provides. The minor irritants can be washed away with solid facts, figures, and case studies, demonstrating the excellence of your firm.

The PR pool can feel like shark-infested waters. Competitive and crowded, with aggressive foes circling for the win. Whether it be diving in with the investors on *Shark Tank* or paddling through the ocean of public relations, success requires preparation, timing and instinct. The best know where and when to feed and how to find opportunities to survive.

They are ready to swim with the sharks.

TOOLBOX TAKEAWAYS

- Learn everything about your audience and where and when to "feed."
- Construct a plan and pitch built on strengths with examples, case studies, and solid results.
- Use storytelling, resulting in a response, "Tell me more," and be prepared to win.

13
PR and Sales: Myth vs. Reality

Can PR increase sales?

Some mistakenly put public relations in the same silo as lead generation or marketing. However, PR stands alone by supporting marketing, rather than duplicating or competing with marketing's efforts. The two perform entirely different functions, yet many believe the goal of a PR campaign is to instantly drive store traffic or generate leads for the sales team.

Many even believe that without a quick return on investment, a public relations effort is wasteful spending.

A case in point, I participated as a guest on a marketing-related podcast, *The Common Cents Show*. Near the end of the hour-long interview the host said, "Let's play a game!"

The host found four short videos on TikTok of people talking about public relations. Based on my 30 years of experience in marketing communications and as a public relations firm owner, he asked me to watch and comment on each and discuss their accuracy.

While three of the four were fairly on target, one totally missed the mark.

The young woman said that unless your public relations campaign is providing you with a fast ROI, and generating revenue, it isn't working and should be dropped immediately.

Obviously, this TikToker did not understand the role of public relations.

It uses strategic communications to build brand recognition, trust, credibility, and mutually beneficial relationships with stakeholders. While marketing's goal is to immediately drive traffic to your website and generate leads—think of public relations as the long game.

PR is a years-long, and in some cases, a decade-long effort to invite audiences to take action and learn more about your company and products. It's an invitation to look under the corporate hood, kick the tires, and see if you're a good fit for a potential business relationship.

When used with media relations it can provide a third-party endorsement of your business. It is not just a company or individual saying they are "great" but the newspaper, magazine, social platform, or television station saying you are "great."

Can PR generate new customers?

Though not its intent, it surely can. Campaigns launched at the right time can certainly open the door to new opportunities—fostering meaningful connections and driving growth.

Such was the case with a fast-growing architectural firm that we partnered with. Through our media relations efforts, the firm was featured in a major daily newspaper—boosting their public image. Concurrently, the architects were pursuing a contract to design a new school.

The selection committee hired our client for the project.

While the architects were qualified to do the work, the owner of firm told me the committee had seen the recent article and commented, "If they are good enough for the newspaper, they are good enough for us." The well-timed article built credibility for the firm, ensured confidence with the committee, and opened the door to a new opportunity.

Our firm was also involved in the launch of Amini's Home Rugs and Game Room in Chesterfield, MO, a St. Louis suburb. Through an intense media relations campaign that included special events, celebrity appearances, feature articles on the business and the owner, awards, and television coverage—the company developed a large client base.

A few years later, Amini's has grown and continues to thrive.

I can point to other examples where interviews and articles helped clients sell books, seminar tickets, IT software and services, safety glasses, custom made men's suits, and more. All helping to grow their client base.

Yet, the framework for a successful campaign takes planning, execution, analysis and standards for measurement. Once launched, the goals of a campaign are much different than those of an advertising strategy or lead generation effort.

An immediate sales-oriented call to action fits into the marketing realm—not PR.

Public relations builds brand and reputation for both the short and long term. Over time, it helps tilt future competitive sales situations in your favor. It lays the groundwork for a company to build on its reputation as a good community citizen—while inspiring confidence and pride in the sales staff and the entire team.

Although there are many lead-generating tools such as purchasing ads, enhancing SEO, and buying lists of prospects—public relations is not one of them. Those that are told a PR plan will provide a quick boost to sales are being misled, and will be greatly disappointed.

PR's goal is not to ask for the sale, but to earn the right to have the conversation.

TOOLBOX TAKEAWAYS

- PR is not lead-gen, marketing, or sales.
- PR builds impact long term.
- PR inspires confidence creating a mutually beneficial conversation.

14
Thought Leadership

Expertise. Insight. Influence. Passion.

Are you a thought leader?

The term is widely used—perhaps overused—in the PR profession to position an individual or company as an expert in a specific field or industry.

An article on LinkedIn defined a thought leader as "One who generates innovative ideas, insight and opinions and then shares them with others. The goal is to influence, inspire and lead the industry or community. A true thought leader should stand out based on their in-depth knowledge, fresh insights, and ability to influence others."

Individuals develop their thought leadership reputation over time. They write books, pen long-form articles in trade and industry journals, serve as a guest on podcasts and industry forums, and depending on their focus, appear on news broadcasts and in feature articles.

CEOs of large corporations fit this genre. Think Apple's Tim Cook, Berkshire Hathaway's Warren Buffet, Sam Altman of Open AI, and Tesla's Elon Musk to name a few.

They talk. People listen.

College professors are highly regarded thought leaders. Many spend hours on specific research and, depending on their status, turn their findings into articles and white papers.

Some can attain near-celebrity status, becoming a sought-after guest for 24-hour news stations and other media platforms.

The educator not only helps build their own brand but that of their university.

Medical professionals also share the leadership role, often revealing the findings of a breakthrough study or research. A physician, by nature of their education and work, is already held in higher regard than the mainstream. Issuing news on a potential cure or drug, benefits his or her personal brand and that of the hospital or research facility.

Similarly, business owners can use thought leadership to build a competitive advantage.

They can shape opinion about their brand and company by submitting articles for trade journals. They can speak at industry events and leverage their expertise for articles and interviews.

Thought Leadership

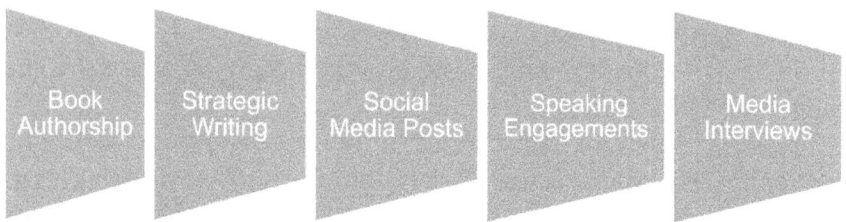

Book Authorship

It seems like everyone is writing a book or has written one. Yet a published treatise with solid business information can elevate your authority and that of your company.

Your name alone on the book cover can take your brand to another level.

I have seen the tone of a conversation change when one describes their authorship of a new book. A word of caution—the book needs to be of value to the reader. It can be short or long but must be well-written with information worth reading.

The book can be of the "how-to" variety or a memoir of lessons learned and industry tips (such as this one).

It can be leveraged to generate other media opportunities such as podcasts, used as a leave-behind as part of a sales call, utilized to help gain speaking engagements, or sold at seminars.

Chapters of the book can also supply the content needed for long-form articles in trade publications, blogs, white papers, and short form posts on social media. It has great value in not only elevating your brand and business but serving as a multifaceted marketing and PR tool.

Strategic Writing

Publishing white papers or long-form articles not only highlight the writer's knowledge and expertise but also serve as a good learning source for others in the field.

White papers are designed to address a specific problem and then offer a solution. They help the reader understand a complex issue with an in-depth analysis. Many are 2,500 words or more. They are best placed in industry trade journals.

Long-form articles provide clarity and depth to a current issue. They are shorter than white papers and are often placed as an op-ed piece with newspapers and business publications

All writings can be used as part of a media kit to generate higher-end media coverage and speaking engagements. Proper placement on the company website also adds to one's depth as an industry expert.

Short Postings on Social Media

Frequent postings on LinkedIn or other channels can be highly beneficial for those seeking greater industry recognition. Comments on trends, opinions on new products, or placement of your photo or video at a key trade show can help elevate your status.

However, flooding social media channels with off-topic content should be avoided. It can send mixed messages to your audience and do more harm than good.

Linking and posting your articles will serve as a conduit for those who wish to read more while optimizing your content.

Speaking Engagements

Thought leaders are featured at forums, seminars, and webinars.

They share their expertise at panel discussions, breakout sessions and keynote speeches. Talks are tailored to the audience, whether it be a general business gathering or a more focused industry-specific meeting. Depending on type and size, many of these gatherings are publicized to a national membership.

Speakers benefit from the publicity before, during, and after the conference.

These events enable the speaker to not only demonstrate their knowledge but also hoist their brand and company.

Podcasts

Podcast interviews are used by thought leaders to promote themselves, their company, and in the case of authors—sell books. They are long-form interviews, usually 30 minutes to one hour, providing the opportunity to delve deeply into a subject.

A multitude of podcasts exist on nearly every subject matter. New ones seem to pop up daily.

The ones with the largest of audiences, think *The Joe Rogan Experience, How I Built This With Guy Raz,* and *The Tim Ferris Show*, are extremely selective about their guests. One must have accomplished something highly significant and already achieved a bit of celebrity hood to warrant consideration.

While the chances of landing an interview on a top tier program are slim, many industry-specific podcasts can provide a solid vehicle to upgrade your brand. These podcasts can be directed at startup entrepreneurs, seasoned business owners, and niche categories such as e-commerce, finance, healthcare, manufacturing, marketing, technology, and more.

As podcasts become an increasingly key part of the media relations mix, the chapter that follows is dedicated to this powerful platform.

Do you have what it takes to be a thought leader—shaping the conversations, influencing the audience, and leading from the front? Thought leadership plays a key role in establishing yourself as an influencer and leader. It enables you to demonstrate your expertise, provide information of high value to your audience and build your brand.

The thought leader understands that when they speak, the audience is always listening.

TOOLBOX TAKEAWAYS

- Thought Leadership elevates your brand and creates new opportunities.
- Many tools can be used that best fit your personality and connects with the targeted audience.
- Plan for consistency and realize long-term benefits.

15
Podcast Power

Have you been on a podcast lately?

From entertainers to authors to business gurus, hundreds use this fast-growing medium to connect with their audience.

So can you.

Podcasts help break through the clutter of daily social media posts and offer an expansive forum to help demonstrate your expertise and elevate your brand. They are one of the fastest growing communication tools and play an important role in a media relations strategy. These interviews can help with overall branding, new product releases, new book releases, and serve as a vehicle for thought leadership.

I have helped clients secure many podcast interviews and appeared as a guest on several, discussing trends in marketing and public relations. The benefit is the guest receives ample time to deliver their message to an attentive group who have chosen to download, watch, and listen.

Podcast appearances offer many benefits of high value.

Connects with a Targeted Audience

Yes, audience size is important. However, quality beats quantity. The challenge is to find the podcast that best matches your intent and interest of the listener.

Unless you're already a celebrity, a best-selling author, or host your own highly rated podcast, the top shows are probably out of reach. And they may not be the best fit overall. Top podcasts seek guests with hundreds of thousands of followers on social media—those who can add to their own group of listeners.

Since hundreds of podcasts exist fitting dozens of genres, finding several in your niche can provide a better return on your time and efforts.

A highly skilled engineer may have a message or story that best fits an engineering-related podcast. Someone who was the victim of a crime, or wrote about one, can find an opportunity with several crime related shows. The creator of a new product for babies will be well served with podcasts geared for new and young mothers.

Those confused about searching out podcast opportunities can subscribe to a service that highlights guest requests. They detail information about each program including audience size, number of programs, and host background. Some are fee-based, and others are no-charge newsletters.

Creators use their podcasts to build their own brand, create leads for their own services, or as a quid pro quo to leverage guests who also have their own podcast, with the goal of appearing on their program.

Shapes the Brand

Podcasts offer long interviews, often 30-60 minutes, that enable you to provide in-depth analysis on key topics—delivering your talking points virtually unedited.

The guest can steer the focus of the interview and provide interesting stories to support any information they wish to communicate. Since many podcasts are aired on YouTube as well as audio channels, there is the opportunity to add a visual element to the interview.

Proper lighting, solid audio equipment, and a few props will help enhance the guest's appearance and the results.

Hosts will showcase the guest's website, book, blog, and other key information the interviewee wishes to promote.

Adds Credibility

A podcast guest gains trust and credibility with the audience. They not only demonstrate knowledge in their area of expertise but can also showcase their personality. The interviewee strengthens their reputation and expands their influence as an industry expert and leader.

This includes highlighting stories to inform and even delight the listener. The goal is to provide impetus for the audience to learn more about the individual and their business.

This can require preparation and, for best results, some assistance from a media training professional.

Promotional Value

One of the big benefits of appearing on a podcast is the promotional value.

Many hosts will heavily publicize each program. This includes highlighting their guests on multiple social platforms—ones the interviewee might not usually target or where they only have a limited following.

Guests can publicize their appearance as well. They can post links on all their social channels, add a link to their website, highlight it in the company newsletter, and use some of the key discussion points to form the foundation for a blog or separate posting.

Provides Long-Tail Benefits

Creators continually post their new podcasts to their online library. They usually do not delete older ones. A guest's recorded interview can be downloaded for months, years, or longer.

They are available for the pleasure of the audience.

Some hosts will maintain live links to the podcast. Your appearance builds your brand for the long term, an added benefit that can pay dividends.

Well beyond the first interview, the guest receives increased visibility resulting in future opportunities. Listeners connect with your voice and values. Social sharing boosts exposure and recommendations.

Should You Host A Podcast?

Podcast hosting is a separate endeavor. It is a more direct route to establishing oneself as an expert in one's field.

A podcast host can determine the subject area or niche they wish to address. Once established, potential guests will contact them, and the host can select whomever they wish to interview.

The host can also aim for the stars and pursue the most well-known authorities in their industry.

The recognizability of the interviewee can help the host increase audience size and build a following. It can lead to sponsorships and become a profit center unto its own.

Consistency is the key to using the podcast as a brand building tool.

Most of the highly downloaded programs are aired daily or weekly. The owner must determine how much time and effort to allocate and how much value the podcast will generate. They need to ascertain whether they have the skills to serve as a host and interviewer.

Consideration must be given to allocating time for selection and coordination of guest appearances, the amount of research necessary for each interview, the hour(s) to record the program, editing, and the time involved in posting and promoting each episode.

Services are available to help in the process. Depending on your budget, they can provide the podcast platform, assistance in locating and scheduling guests, promotion, and alleviating wasted time and energy.

Still, as one who hosted his own radio show, it would be prudent to allocate a minimum of three hours for each podcast.

Podcast Success Story

Our firm has had the privilege of working with Paul Bruno, an author who writes books about an American icon—the Jeep. His focus is on early Jeep history and the book, *The Original Jeeps*, details how this special automobile came into existence for use in World War II. It highlights the politicians, military personnel, and automobile manufacturers involved in the process.

The Jeep brand is well-known to millions of car enthusiasts, but the competition to design and manufacture the first vehicle was an important chapter of both American and military history.

Bruno is an excellent storyteller and had a solid career in project management. He could easily speak to audiences of divergent interests.

We helped him create and execute a podcast strategy under the media relations umbrella.

This involved not only targeting Jeep fans, but also general automotive audiences, military buffs, World War II aficionados, American history enthusiasts, engineering shows, and programs based on new book releases.

Many of the interviews were highly effective in helping Bruno establish himself as a thought leader about Jeeps and related military history. They drove traffic to his page on Amazon and other sellers, sold books, and created additional opportunities. His model of addressing different genres helped secure a variety of appearances, as he built authority and credibility.

The work provides a good case study of how to utilize podcasts as part of an overall PR campaign.

Whether you're a guest on a podcast or venturing into new waters to host your own, podcasts are a powerful marketing tool with a long tail. With the right preparation and strategy, podcast appearances can boost your brand. For many you can become the voice your industry seeks out.

And soon you may find others asking not if you've been on a podcast—but which one.

TOOLBOX TAKEAWAYS

- Podcasts are an excellent marketing tool to build a brand and thought leadership.
- Search out podcasts that best fit your expertise and niche audience.
- Think out of the box and explore all genres where your book, background and expertise would be a welcome fit.
- Depending on your goals, consider hosting a podcast for more control of your brand and message.

16
Are You a Lion or a Gazelle?

"Every morning in Africa, a gazelle wakes up; it knows it must outrun the fastest lion, or it will be killed. Every morning in Africa, a lion wakes up. It knows it must run faster than the slowest gazelle, or it will starve. It doesn't matter whether you're the lion or a gazelle—when the sun comes up, you'd better be running."

This quote, often attributed to Christopher McDougall in his book *Born to Run: A Hidden Tribe, Superathletes, and the Greatest Race the World Has Never Seen,* can be applied to those involved in the daily battles of marketing and public relations

Several years ago, I attended a seminar and the speaker used this parable as the foundation for his speech. He likened the story to what happens daily in sales and marketing.

Paraphrasing, he said as the anointed hunter of his family, the lead lion realizes his family will not eat until a gazelle is brought back to the den. The lion will chase his prey from sunup to sundown until the job is done. He does not care how hot it is, how many miles he has traveled, or how fast the pack of gazelles is running. Unless that lion can apprehend their prey, he realizes his family will starve and he will have let them down.

Meanwhile, the gazelle's goal is only to avoid the lion. Once the gazelle realizes he won't be caught, he can relax. He can eat some plants, drink whatever water he can find, and spend the rest of the day lounging—waiting for the next sunrise.

The speaker related this scenario to those in the selling world and there is sound advice here for those in PR.

Are you a PR lion? Are you up early with a strategy in mind, ready to pursue the next client—or elevate the brand of an existing client? Will you push past the barriers and daily distractions, blocking out the noise of competitors? Will you let nothing stop you in the pursuit of feeding your agency family as well as your own?

Or…are you a gazelle? Happy to maintain the status quo, while dodging a few pitfalls and doing just enough to last another day.

The PR lion is the one who is driven to succeed. They are an innovator, not afraid to step out of the box—trying new strategies, new tactics, and utilizing innovative thinking to outpace competitors.

Lions learn new technologies to benefit their clients, their agency, and in the long term, themselves.

PR lions study the impact of AI and how it can be beneficial in the public relations process. They expertly detail their findings in a format that helps their coworkers and clients.

PR lions spend extra time learning the nuances of media relations and connecting with journalists, influencer marketing, event creation, and new social media forums. They take classes and work beyond normal business hours.

They are first in line to take on more responsibility. First in line to receive a promotion.

On the other side of the fence, the PR gazelle is happy in the current landscape, doing the bare minimum to get by, staying the normal course. They wait for someone to give them more responsibility which may never come.

Their hope is to just hang around and last another year.

PR lions tend to dominate their industry, set the bar high, and eagerly gear up each day to do it all over again. PR gazelles play the waiting game, focusing mainly on survival. Over time, these gazelles tend to get eaten alive by the lions—getting swallowed up by the competition.

Which one are you?

TOOLBOX TAKEAWAYS

- PR Lions are leaders of the pack trending to dominate their agency or business.
- Lions hunt until they get the job done.
- PR Gazelles exist to feed the lions and get eaten alive by the competition.

17
Wordsmithing: A Superpower

Is there one superpower that can elevate your agency and career?

The art of wordsmithing is certainly a skill of high value. One that can help a PR professional stand out from the crowd.

A wordsmith possesses the ability to take complex strategic positions and craft them into short, concise, and perhaps memorable statements. It is what separates great writers from the pack.

This is especially applicable in today's digital environment where unique selling propositions appear in short word bursts on Facebook, Instagram, LinkedIn, TikTok, and other social media.

Consider these slogans:

> *Bounty: The Quicker Picker Upper*
> *L'Oreal: Because You're Worth It*
> *State Farm: Like A Good Neighbor, State Farm Is There*
> *Taco Bell: Think Outside The Bun*

They position the brand while fostering recognition with a broad audience and an affinity with a targeted audience.

How do these successful catchphrases apply to PR professionals?

Think beyond standard news releases and email pitches. Focus on messaging that can raise the temperature of the reader, rises above the noise, and spurs a journalist, customer, or stakeholder to take action concerning your business or client.

I use five general rules when tasked with a writing assignment. These can help whenever your talents as a wordsmith are put to the test.

Think of News Releases as Advertising
Go beyond the usual platitudes and research the words and phrases *customers* use to describe your client's product benefits.

Gain access to salespeople or those who interface with customers. They are a good source of this type of information.

Grab these golden nuggets. Go beyond keywords. Demonstrate your company's value in clear, concise statements.

Learn the Value of the Client's Product and State It

Does the product or service solve a particular problem? Are you communicating those details succinctly in your messaging? Every company has a list of product benefits. Learn to state them in a way a journalist or targeted producer will not only notice them, but find them interesting.

> *"Acme's drain cleaner works in seconds, at half the price of other brands. It's no wonder the company has grown 50% in the last year and is on a trajectory to double that in the next two years."*

Tell a Story

Good PR begins with good storytelling.

Instead of telling them how great a client's product works, drive home that message with an example of how a client helped a company or individual with a specific solution for their problem.

Instead of just "Smith Services provides money saving solutions for companies in various industries such as ...," focus on one or two instances of how Smith impacted a community or targeted audience.

Mary Jones in Joplin, MO said, "Following the tornado, several homes needed immediate repair. Smith rushed in with a full crew. I was amazed how quickly their design and construction team made those homes livable again."

How you write it and tell it will put your storytelling abilities to the test.

Adjust for Different Audiences

Channels differ based on audience demographics.

How you present your client's story can be tailored for each individual medium.

Some may be longer form. Editors may prefer expanded content and messages with case studies and additional detail. Others, in-line with shorter social media styled publications, may rely on videos and photos. Those should be included as needed. No matter the vehicle, the undertone of key words and phrases should remain the same. The goal is to speak to each journalist individually, maintaining consistency and competitive differentiation.

Test for Best Results

A typical advertising campaign begins with focus groups, surveys, and other methods of customer feedback. Responses are used to determine the path of the planned campaign; whether initial findings are verified, or a new direction is necessary.

Some phrases work better than others.

From a public relations perspective, different versions of messaging can be created and used with small audiences. Results can be measured to determine those providing the best results. Two sets of pitches can be sent to different reporters. One, in all likelihood, will generate the best response and can be modeled going forward.

Messaging in white papers and newsletters can be compared for responses and any resulting calls to action.

A small change, such as adjusting one word in a sentence, can often lead to big results.

Wordsmithing is a superpower that can elevate your agency as well as your career. Learning how to successfully shape the message can help dominate the competition. Your message won't just be heard; it will be felt.

TOOLBOX TAKEAWAYS

- Becoming a better wordsmith can help a PR pro stand out from the crowd.
- Words and messaging should be tailored to each individual journalist yet underlying themes should remain the same for branding consistency.
- Creative storytelling can highlight how a client's product solves a problem with an innovative solution.
- The better the story, the better the results.

18
The Press Release: Why It Still Matters

General Douglas MacArthur once said, "Old soldiers never die, they just fade away."

Concluding his Army tenure, he was describing the departure of an individual from a significant role rather than their literal death.

The press release can be considered an "old solider" of the public relations militia, one facing its own fading glory. Many public relations journals and newsletters have highlighted the presumptive death of the press release.

Once the industry standard for communicating news with journalists and stakeholders, these formatted communiques are said to be slowly finding their way to the PR tactical retirement home. Surely, as a media pitching tool, they are becoming less relevant and must be condensed and reformatted in emails to better serve busy and time-starved editors and producers.

Still the press release has value.

It is required for issuing financial news from publicly traded corporations and formal announcements from government and other entities. They provide depth and analysis to accompany short-form media blasts.

Press releases provide utility as a mechanism to improve search engine optimization (SEO).

Many online news sources will post a company's press release at little to no charge. Businesses can use these to improve keyword rankings on AI, Google, Bing, and other search engines.

The press release still retains great merit in its structure. Its inverted pyramid approach enables the writer to organize their thoughts and highlight the key points of the news to be issued.

For those unaware, or for those who have simply forgotten, its format is basic and succinct.

The Lead
Who? What? When? Where? Why?

The Body
Argument, Evidence, Expert Quotes

The Tail
More Content

Boilerplate
Conclusive Ending

The first paragraph immediately following the headline is the "lead" or "lede". It is the most important part of the release. It includes the Who, What, When, Where, Why, and How of the news. The basis for the news release is included in this paragraph. Occasionally, the lead can be expanded to a second paragraph. A special public event, such as a parade, festival, or gathering for a social cause, would highlight the basics of the information in this paragraph including the event's name, day, and time.

The lead funnels into the body. This is where more details and expert quotes can be applied to support the lead. For example, expanding information about a special event can include the reason for the event, anticipated attendance or crowd, and a quote from the organizer.

Following is the tail, with more background and expanded content. It includes more items the journalist will find interesting such as history of the event, details on attendance growth, and quotes from past attendees.

Finally comes the concluding paragraph or "boilerplate." This is a corporate governance declaration describing the organization's mission and any copyrighted material regarding brand name. The website address and/or phone number is often listed. The name and information for the media contact person is also displayed either at the top or bottom of the release.

Even the best constructed press release faces challenges in today's fast-paced digital climate. Surely, a one-size fits all approach is ineffective. Each release must be adapted to the individual needs of the journalist or medium.

Why?

In an era of shrinking newsrooms, reporters have little time to cull through the horde of daily emails much less a battery of long press releases. They may be tasked with not only writing stories but also creating a blog, shooting video, and appearing on podcasts.

I have attended many interviews and seminars with editors, newspaper reporters, and producers. They all indicate the need for speed. Reporters tell public relations professionals to initially forgo length and send short informational blasts. Still, they must not only be informative, but also on point with daily coverage needs. Emphasis should be given to the email subject line which must grab their attention.

The golden nuggets from the press release can be excavated into short concise sentences. They should be placed in the body of the email. Bullet points can be used to make the narrative easier to scan. Links can be included to other more detailed sources of information such as a video or media kit.

The goal is to ensure it gets to the journalist's inbox without obstruction from a fire wall.

Journalists will contact the PR person should the information be on point. They may ask for more details or desire to speak directly to the CEO or those quoted in the email.

Shorter press releases can also be posted directly to social channels. They expand the reach of the targeted audience.

Like an old soldier, the press release may have lost its ranking in PR command but still offers structure and organization. Rather than simply casting it aside, press releases can provide front line support to any battle, helping a campaign emerge victorious.

TOOLBOX TAKEAWAYS

- Standard press releases still provide structure and organization.
- Press release nuggets can be extracted into shorter email blasts.
- Shorter press releases can be posted directly on social media.

19
Mastering Response Time

In today's high-tech world, one glitch, one misstep, can trigger a ripple felt around the world.

On July 19, 2024, at 10:30 a.m., I got a call from a reporter at the NBC affiliate in St. Louis. CrowdStrike Holdings, a large cybersecurity company listed on the NASDAQ exchange, had caused a worldwide computer outage.

Attempting to automatically update computers, it created a misfire and caused screens to go blank. It shut down thousands of operating systems, rendering them useless.

Microsoft estimated 8.5 million devices were affected.

This failure grounded airplanes, cut off access to many banking systems, and disrupted major healthcare networks. It threw at least one news network off the air.

The journalist wanted comments from one of our clients, ThrottleNet, a local IT and cybersecurity firm. Realizing the importance of media coverage in a competitive IT market, I quickly sprang into action and reached George Rosenthal, ThrottleNet's President. He was leaving for a short trip—bags packed and dogs in his vehicle. Realizing the importance of these rare media opportunities, Rosenthal said he would reschedule his plans and make it happen.

Rosenthal, experienced with TV and radio interviews, drove quickly to the station. He appeared live on the Noon news, and was asked about the outage and what it meant for those traveling on airlines, banking with ATMs, and medical appointments.

His comments were on point, in terms everyone could understand, and well received.

He was on the newscast for five minutes—unheard of on live local television—and then was asked to appear again on the 12:30 p.m. news. He was on camera even longer. The interview lasted nearly seven minutes, breaking his earlier "record" of five minutes.

The CrowdStrike failure was major news and Rosenthal was on a verbal roll, dispensing technical information in laymen's terms.

The team at KSDK seized the opportunity and put Rosenthal on live again at 4pm. Then live at 6pm. The news team also interviewed him separately on video and included some of his comments on the 10pm News.

The interview was posted on the KSDK website and remained for several days. All told Rosenthal spent some seven hours embedded at the TV station, providing over 20 minutes of news coverage.

While he was at the station he also carved out time to do two additional radio interviews.

This paramount effort strengthened Rosenthal's reputation as a thought leader in IT and cybersecurity, and enhanced ThrottleNet's positioning as a knowledgeable, skilled technology firm worthy of serving businesses throughout the region.

The video clips served as excellent content for social media. Interviews and links were highlighted on several of ThrottleNet's channels, their website, and in emails.

None of this would have been possible if Rosenthal simply said he was busy or said he couldn't travel to the station.

Though rare, similar opportunities can arise for any business or organization. Leaders should be prepared to take advantage of these fast deadline media requests. Rosenthal's high-profile media day illustrates how quick actions in an unexpected crisis present a powerful opportunity. Here's what worked, and what any leader or PR professional needs to respond and navigate these unexpected moments:

Keep Essential Contact Info on Hand

PR reps should have cell phone numbers, emails, and the name of an assistant who can help track down the potential interviewee. The spokesperson should be aware that an interview request is a possibility at times of a related breaking news event. They should maintain flexibility in their scheduling or have a second person on the team able to appear. The goal is to enable a quick response rather than lose the opportunity to a competitor.

Invest in Media Training

The TV opportunity was successful due to Rosenthal's experience as an interviewee. He had appeared on dozens of radio and TV interviews prior to the daylong appearance and felt a high degree of comfort in front of the camera and microphone. Leaders who desire similar coverage should invest in media training. The objective is to not only handle the stress of the bright lights but communicate as an industry leader, building confidence with the audience. Proper dress and posture are a necessity. An additional staff person might also take part in the training and serve as a second resource should the CEO be unable to appear.

Educate Yourself on the Subject Matter

In this case, Rosenthal was able to do a quick study of corresponding events that day. He read news reports and watched videos from newscasts. Already well-educated on the variances of cybersecurity, he was able to communicate knowledgeably on the subject. Should he had been ill-prepared, the first interview may have had less impact and he may not have been invited to appear on the other programs. CEOs should be well-read and highly prepared to comment when opportunities present themselves.

Public relations professionals should work with leadership to ensure they are ready and able to handle any breaking news media request. It can result in a large gain in influence, thought leadership, and open the doors for additional media opportunities.

Not everyone will have a chance to respond to a crisis that sends shockwaves around the globe. Yet the ability to handle the unexpected media opportunity is what sets you apart from the rest.

TOOLBOX TAKEAWAYS

- When a media opportunity comes knocking be ready to open the door and open it fast.
- Ensure the CEO and others are media trained to handle TV interviews on short notice.
- Prepare the spokesperson for the necessary time commitment to meet the demands of the station.

20
Oscar Worthy Award Strategies

Turn on the lights.
Cue the applause.
And the award goes to...

Your company, provided you are Oscar ready and worthy.

Industry awards serve as a powerful tool to strengthen brand image and generate publicity. Externally, they drive awareness, ignite influence, and spark media buzz. Internally, they serve as a dynamic conduit for team building, energize recruitment efforts, and fuel overall excitement when the award is announced.

One of the most gratifying roles in public relations is helping a client accomplish something truly out of the ordinary. This achievement often takes the form of a distinguished award—earned through outstanding individual or company performance.

I have guided many clients in their pursuit of prestigious top-tier national and local awards. Some for their exemplary corporate success, others for individual achievement and outstanding community impact.

Many clients have been fortunate to win these special accolades. Some even received coverage as a finalist.

A crowning achievement for one client was receiving the *Forbes* Small Giant Award. *Forbes* magazine saluted Cohen Woodworking for intentional long-term growth and performance, its company culture, and its role as a solid citizen of the community it serves.

Many businesses understand the value of these awards and the creation of an annual strategy to attain them. Yet many small and medium-sized firms fail to pursue these golden PR nuggets.

They either do not grasp the concept, do not allocate the time to complete the documents required, or simply do not make it a key part of their marketing efforts.

Years of insight reveal five key strategies any company can utilize in crafting a plan for earning these special honors—and, once earned, maximize their impact.

Commit to a Strategic Awards Strategy

This requires a proactive approach. One that includes research and determining which awards will be most beneficial in brand growth, influence and relationship building.

For many companies, large, national honors, such as the Inc. 5000, may be the only one's worth chasing. For others, local awards, such as Fastest Growing Companies, Top Accounting Firm, Best Places To Work etc., can offer a high level of prestige and be notable with current clients and prospects.

Awards—No Strings Attached

Nearly all reputable awards are given out at no cost or require a small, affordable entry fee. However, some ask for a hefty sum just for consideration.

While the sponsoring company certainly incurs some costs with processing and judging applications, those with seemingly excessive fees should be avoided.

Many unknown organizations practically proclaim you have already been named the top company in your category—and for a fee of $800, will secure your listing and send you a nice trophy. For an additional fee, they will feature you in one of their magazines. In the long run, these meaningless honors have no value for you or your clients.

Designate an Awards Ambassador

> Applications pushed to the bottom of the pile.
> Deadlines missed.
> Regrets ensue after another missed opportunity.

Businesses can avoid disappointment by designating a point person to be an awards ambassador. The individual can seek out award opportunities in-line with the company's mission, messaging, and values. They can be charged with ensuring all necessary paperwork is readily available.

The point person could be a member of the marketing department or administrative team. They should be provided with access to whatever information is needed to complete each entry.

Share Your Success

Some companies will spend hours working on an awards application then bury the news once they receive their special honor. They place their plaque or trophy on a shelf in the lobby, then forget about it.

The business owner should ensure that all members of the team share in their success.

The award should be shown and highlighted during a company meeting. Those most responsible for attaining the award should be recognized. News of the award should be posted on the company website and included in the newsletter.

The award can serve as a vehicle to build team camaraderie, enhance prestige, improve employee satisfaction, and create a buzz throughout the organization.

Leverage Your Recognition for Optimal Branding and Publicity

Most awarding organizations will attempt to highlight their honored companies. Usually this occurs through a listing in the event program, an ad in a publication, tickets to an awards banquet, or a template news release sent to winners to distribute to their local media. However, businesses should escalate those efforts.

Winning companies can post the news of the award—and the accompanying photo and/or video—on their website and all viable social media channels. Company formatted news releases should be created and distributed to the local media, business publications, and trade journals.

News of the award can be highlighted in an email sent to clients. An award badge or line of recognition can be added to email signature lines. A story surrounding how the team made the accomplishment happen provides excellent content for the company blog and newsletter.

Winning an award represents commitment, dedication and execution at a high level. Yet chasing an award simply for the sake of securing a top honor is a trap to be avoided. Organizations can lose focus of why they do their work in the first place. They should avoid pursuing one award then quickly move on to pursue another. Focusing on performing above and beyond expectations will yield greater results, ones that are worthy of top recognition.

Prestigious awards not only elevate the company in the minds of its employees and clients but also serve as an attractive recruiting tool. Organizations receive the kind of industry recognition that produces great public relations value—both internally and externally. It can reinforce your position as a solid business partner and provide gravitas to those considering your business for engagement.

It creates excitement throughout the organization and rivals the exuberance of an actor winning an academy award. That type of energy will set your company apart. Now cue the applause.

TOOLBOX TAKEAWAYS

- Awards help elevate your brand both internally and externally.
- For best results, businesses should commit to a strategic awards strategy.
- All honors should be shared with your team and the community you serve.

21
Choosing The Right PR Firm—Be Selective

What happens when you hire the wrong PR firm?

I have heard many businesses owners complain about their public relations agency. They utter disappointment about the lack of performance in line with company goals and the expensive continuation of service.

Together, the agency and organization devote vast amounts of time developing effective messaging and crafting winning strategies. The business invests substantial sums into campaign execution—only to see lackluster results.

The PR firm's leadership team—instrumental in landing the company's business and believed to be masterminding the campaign—shifts its focus to other revenue-generating activities. They leave day-to-day account management in the hands of less experienced and less knowledgeable personnel, much to the shortfall of the client. Frustrated with questionable results, the business decides to switch agencies. They invite other firms to submit proposals, meet with several, and select a replacement.

A successful business-agency partnership begins with the corporate CEO or key marketing person, and their perceived expectations. Challenges ensue when an owner miscalculates the value of their brand and the time and effort needed to elevate it. Some hire the largest agency, believing their small company will get the same attention and results as large national brands. The prestige of working with a large international agency—with their vast stable of offices, consultants, and support-staff—comes at a high cost.

One unsustainable by most in the long term.

Business needs and budgets can vary greatly depending on their goals. Factors include the location and number of customers to be targeted, and market segmentation. Many companies are best suited to engage with smaller agencies, perhaps one with specialization in their business niche. Others are best suited for a regional firm with a wealth of media connections in a certain trade area.

Smaller costs may not yield smaller results. In fact, the opposite is often the case.

Choosing the right agency that fits your needs, and budget involves five key factors. Understanding these will not only help secure a good partnership but also drive results.

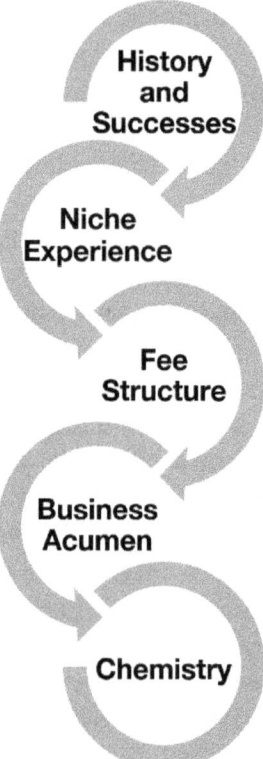

Documented History and Success

Not knowing an agency's history can be a risk to your future.

Business owners would never trust the inner workings of their company with an accountant or attorney with one or two years of experience. The same holds true for an agency partner.

Organizations should seek out longevity and ask for results generated on behalf of other agency clients. The agency should have a general understanding of business operations and the functional aspect of how branding can impact a company's image and sales.

Agency executives should have a list of clients and their case studies readily available. References are also helpful.

A list of agency awards and accolades is also a good indication of how an agency approaches its own branding and provides hints as to how they would handle yours.

Niche Experience

Do you need an entire army of PR professionals or a few seasoned veterans to reach your goals?

Consider a football team. They have "specialists" for different aspects of the game, whether it be offense, defense, or special teams.

Many agencies also have specialized expertise. Some in select business genres.

One may be well schooled in working with technology-related companies; another may do well with retail brands. Still others may be focused on hospitality and travel, construction, or the financial industry.

A smaller firm with a wealth of experience in a targeted market segment can be a valuable partner—a much better fit than a large agency with a smattering of clients in different industries.

Clients should consider firms who understand their business model and customers, and who work with targeted journalists within their field.

Fee Structure

Look beyond the sticker price. Understand the price tag. Focus not just on hours but impact.

Most agencies work on a retainer basis. This is a monthly fee based on the man-hours and resources needed to execute the campaign. These fees are dependent on the length of the campaign.

Some businesses require ongoing support while others only need short-term engagement. As a rule of thumb, three to six months for the planning and execution of a special event or project with a short turnaround is acceptable. Long-term campaigns may require a one-year or two-year commitment.

Some agencies may operate strictly by charging an hourly fee. Utilizing this model, a business can expect to pay more during periods of intense work and less when activity is limited.

Others may charge a hybrid fee where a small retainer is implemented to guarantee a few hours of work per month. Any additional work is billed at an agreed hourly rate.

By fine tuning their focus, business owners can select an agency to help them achieve their goals and do so at a fee well within their budget.

Business Acumen

Brand messaging means nothing when the business plan isn't understood. It is only effective when the firm understands the client's vision. Otherwise, the campaign falls flat.

"Full-service" firms often miss the mark. They offer a boatload of services such as digital marketing, website design, content building, and oh yes—media relations.

In my experience few, if any, of these one-size-fits-all agencies have succeeded in landing top-tier PR results. They offer public relations in the same way a restaurant provides an additional topping of mushrooms to a well-cooked ribeye. They design graphically attractive websites but lack the know-how of incorporating business positioning and messaging into online communications. They outsource work to a writer or freelancer who may not have the knowledge or experience to assist the business with proper planning, strategy, and measurement.

Agencies should have the wherewithal to understand the client's business operations, brand messaging, and the ability to create a results-oriented strategic plan with the expertise on-board to execute it.

Chemistry

While blending the right elements is essential to PR success, mixing the wrong elements can lead to an explosive reaction.

Business leaders should look to an agency team that shares their beliefs, values, and in many cases, their individual interests. They will spend a great amount of time together not just planning the campaign launch but working in tandem as the effort continues.

Confidence, trust, and likeability should be apparent. Conversely initial interviews that bring out negativity and second-guessing are clues that the partnership will be unsuccessful.

Business relationships grow when personal stories are shared. Common interests become central parts of the discussion.

We have worked with many companies where the right type of chemistry existed between business ownership and our firm. Many of these relationships have lasted five years, ten years—even 30 years. Many grew into personal friendships with strong bonds. Still the focus needs to be on performance and results.

Clients should think long term. They should select an agency that can yield top-line results with the right chemistry to make it all happen.

TOOLBOX TAKEAWAYS

- Explore partnerships beyond the largest firms to those with specific expertise in your industry.
- Discuss and agree upon expectations prior to firm engagement.
- Select an agency partner with the right experience and right chemistry for optimal results.

22
PR: The Digital Calling Card

Your digital footprint is your calling card to the world. Get it right and you open the door to new connections, new relationships, and new opportunities. Get it wrong and you reduce the perceived value of your business and brand.

The digital footprint includes not only your website, but also various platforms to engage with audiences—think LinkedIn, Instagram, Facebook, and X. This is often the first point of contact between you and potential customers.

They all work in unison like a completed Rubik's cube, where all the rows are properly aligned for top-line results. Some or all are used to build awareness, trust, and credibility. Social channels should be fine-tuned to serve as a driver to the company's website.

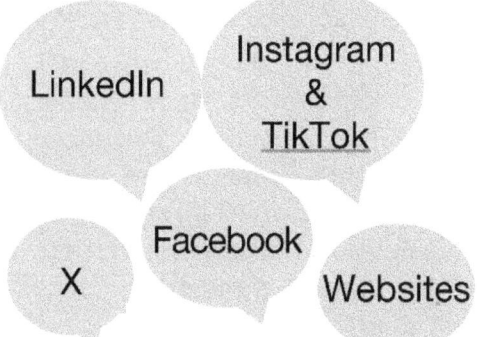

LinkedIn

A professional networking platform, LinkedIn is considered the channel for job hunters. It is that, and more. Consider it as a site within a site to showcase your company.

Corporate pages are a major focus area. News, updates, and links to articles can be posted. Executives can do the same on their personal pages. Corporate messaging can be communicated to tens of thousands of combined connections. Industry groups provide additional outlets for participation. The site is the primary connecting point for those who serve the business-to-business segment. It is ideal for thought leader positioning.

Live links to articles and other information can be posted, which is an excellent branding tool. Hashtags are utilized for additional exposure to targeted groups.

Facebook

In contrast to LinkedIn's professional presence, Facebook focuses more on the retail and personal market. Brands, auto dealers, shop owners, online stores, influencers and restaurants will use the channel to promote their offerings and reach their target audience.

The outlet offers both corporate pages and of course personal pages. Originally used as a tool for daily updates on family, friends, and entertainment, these posts often get overshadowed by business messaging. Additional product promotion can be secured on Facebook Groups or Marketplace. The site permits live links to articles and media placements for added awareness. Livestreams are also used for podcasts and special events.

Instagram/TikTok

Built around photos and short video blasts, these channels engage users with visual content. Many consumer brands use the channel to reach younger audiences. Influencers use the channel to build their personal brand and secure corporate partnerships. Brands and PR professionals must be adept at creating messaging that is not only highly visual but on-point with marketing objectives. Hashtags add to specific groups of interest for additional exposure.

X

A central channel for breaking news, entertainment, politics, and sports updates, X keeps consumers updated around the clock. In many cases postings will precede those of major news outlets as events occur. The site's strength is its timeliness and ability for users to comment on each post. It is highly visual and often controversial.

Benefits include the ability to connect with a variety of journalists and thought leaders. Live links and hashtags can help amplify any posting. Threads and other sites offer similar messaging opportunities.

Websites

Websites are the informational hub for any business or organization—the main point of contact between a company and its customers and prospects.

Think of social media as your foot soldiers, and your website as central command. The soldiers are paving routes for awareness, steering viewers to your site to learn more about the operation and generals (leaders) for a more in-depth brand experience.

The website is a key public relations tool. One that will be explored following any article, TV appearance or media placement. It should be well-designed, well-written, and current to create the desired perception with the audience.

Poorly constructed sites do just the opposite. They counteract any advertising, media relations, or community outreach—resulting in wasted time, wasted money, and a lack of opportunities.

The best websites employ the following:

"Customer Think"
>If you were shopping for an item and visited your website, would you consider purchasing it?

Clear and Concise Offerings
>Position your offerings as a lead headline. Demonstrate how you provide solutions to problems. Focus on corporate messaging. In most cases, company history—often used at the top of the first page—can be detailed later towards the bottom of the scroll.

A Call to Action
>Many businesses will look to immediately engage the visitor with a chat box. Others will provide a free whitepaper or newsletter sign-up form. The goal is to enhance engagement, generate leads, and create relationships.

Ease of Navigation
>Customers search from a variety of devices. Websites must be designed to work within the framework of all platforms whether they be laptops, tablets, iPads, iPhones, or android based. Many sites are structured for desktop or tablet but fail to appear properly on other equipment.

Periodic Updating

Websites should avoid looking stale. Messaging—headlines, taglines, descriptions, style, calls to action, and content—should be updated as needed. New products and new services should be highlighted. Personnel, if included on the site, should reflect current team leaders and eliminate those no longer with the organization. Visitors should see new content and current happenings on the company news page.

Your digital footprint isn't just a buzzword—it's at the core of any public relations campaign. Strong messaging and dynamic visuals should shine not only on your website, but across all your targeted social channels. The right approach ignites awareness, interest, perceived value, and delivers impactful results to both stakeholders and customers.

TOOLBOX TAKEAWAYS

- A business' digital footprint should showcase its brand and highlight its messaging under the umbrella of a public relations campaign.
- Selected social channels should drive traffic to the company's website for additional information and engagement.
- Websites should be well-written, visually appealing, updated regularly and easy-to-navigate across a variety of platforms.

23
Recruiting PR: Taking a Company from Good to Great

Jim Collins, in his best-selling book *Good to Great,* said achieving greatness begins when you have the right people on the bus. People who are capable, passionate, and share the company's core values.

He wrote that a strong team of individuals can adapt to changing circumstances and overcome challenges more effectively than a plan that is well-defined but poorly staffed. The *who* takes precedence over the *what*.

Any strategic plan, no matter how complete or creative, will fail if the right team isn't in place to execute it. The bus gets stuck in neutral and may even slide backwards.

Recruiting focused PR establishes and enhances the company's culture to not only get the right people on the bus but to keep the bus running in high gear. It not only attracts the best candidates but keeps the successful ones on board.

Think in terms of Alphabet-Google, Apple, Coca-Cola, Ford, Goldman Sachs, McKinsey, Nike and Walt Disney.

Though undoubtedly flooded with resumes from high-achieving college graduates and young business professionals, many employ branding strategies strictly for talent acquisition.

The goal is to secure the best of the best, ensuring continued greatness.

These top companies do more than post jobs on their website. They employ creative outreach strategies, launching a host of digital weaponry from their branding arsenal.

Good companies ascending to become great can follow their lead. They can deploy several strategies to establish an emotional foothold as they upscale the pool of potential candidates.

Clear Messaging and Communication

A company's core values should be highlighted in the messaging. It should be clear and easily understandable.

Nike, on its website, says, "There is a sense of pride that comes from representing an iconic brand and shaping its future. "What moves you moves our world". "Here, we treat every day as a new opportunity to push boundaries, ask tough questions and share whole-hearted convictions. We are a team – united by the belief that anything is possible."

The Apple career site says, "We aren't merely creating products. We're creating something magical for the person who uses it."

On its careers site Coca Cola states both its purpose and its vision. "Our Purpose: Refresh the world. Make a difference." "Our Vision is to create the brands and choice of drinks that people love, to refresh them in body & spirit. And done in ways that create a more sustainable business and better shared future that makes a difference in people's lives, communities and our planet."

Businesses on an upward trajectory can craft similar styled messaging that fits their culture and goals. It should be highlighted on career pages and other forms of communication.

Videos on Company Culture

The best companies don't just say it they show it. They connect visually with a generation raised on digital devices and video channels.

Ford highlights its message in a fast-paced careers video, "Movers of the world. Makers of the future." It has videos related to talent acquisition including advice for recent graduates, interview tips from Ford campus recruiters, a message from the CEO and much more.

Many of these videos are not only shared on the careers site but on YouTube, Facebook and more.

Smaller firms may not have the budget or resources of a large conglomerate, but they can still highlight team members focusing on "A Day In The Life" of a recent new hire, record a message from a leader, or use video to highlight a new project.

Securing and Highlighting Media Coverage

Ascending companies should seek out articles, interviews and other forms of media coverage.

The coverage helps brand the business and increases awareness to compete against corporations with household names.

Articles in The Wall Street Journal, Forbes, and other business journals build credibility with candidates. The same for television coverage and other media exposure. In many cases larger local articles are as effective as smaller national placements.

Media placements should be highly valued and placed not only on the company's news page but also on company social channels with thumbnails and links on LinkedIn, Facebook and Instagram, and videos on YouTube.

Social Media Posting

Connecting with today's digital audience requires an aggressive campaign on social media.

Companies should utilize the channels that provide the best results. Postings should be on LinkedIn and in most cases Facebook, and Instagram. YouTube, as highlighted earlier, is one of the fastest growing mediums and videos should be utilized to showcase company culture.

Postings should be consistent and done for the long term. Photos of team members, exciting projects, and other news items can be placed weekly, and in some cases more frequently.

Awards Strategy

Opportunities exist for companies to win awards for maintaining a thriving workplace. Many local business journals and newspapers offer this type of recognition on an annual basis.

Recognition as one of the best places to work in a city or region adds credibility to any recruiting campaign.

Many national publications and industry specific journals offer similar awards.

These awards should be highlighted in all company communication, from the website to newsletter to social posts.

These third-party endorsements provide excellent branding tools to highlight company culture and showcase the benefits of working at your business.

Networking Events

Corporate messaging should be conveyed at selected career events, whether they be on campus or at selected job fairs.

Videos can be played on tablets and other devices. Photos can be displayed within a booth.

Informational brochures and other printed materials can be provided for more in-depth descriptions.

Company representatives should accurately communicate all aspects of a company's culture to further enhance value, transparency and the corporate brand as they meet one-on-one with prospective candidates.

Creating a PR strategy focused on recruiting can play a strong role in upscaling the pool of potential candidates. It should highlight a company culture that communicates a trajectory of growth and opportunity. It can help put the right people on the bus, elevating a good company into a great one.

> **TOOLBOX TAKEAWAYS**
>
> ➢ A PR campaign targeted strictly for recruiting can help a company attract higher levels of candidates and retain top stars.
> ➢ Messaging on company culture should be created and developed and highlighted on the company's website and social media.
> ➢ An outreach effort with consistent postings on social channels will enhance brand and connect with today's digital audience.

24
The Power of the Subject Line

> **From:** *Steve* Turner
> **To:**
> **Subject:** *Rare 1957 Dual-Ghia Convertible Owned by Frank Sinatra Now For Sale at Daniel Schmitt Auto – Potential Story*

Anyone who covers vintage automobiles would certainly be intrigued by that headline.

Throw in a celebrity twist and journalists will be hooked, eager to dig. Many will want to write about it. In fact, they did just that.

The email ignited coverage in multiple publications and TV news—all with photos, and in some cases, video showcasing the vehicle. Offers rolled in.

While not every PR pro has a client selling a $350,000 classic car formerly owned by a movie star, the process of generating coverage for your business, product, or event remains the same. It begins with an email and a strong subject line.

Why?

As newsrooms shrink and budgets decrease, writers face continual pressure to create interesting content. They must do so in a fast-paced digital environment crowded with noise and distractions vying for attention.

Alongside the hectic newsroom, many journalists work from home. Some in settings far removed from their national office. A good number of writers are freelancers, paid by the project. Depending on the publication, they could reside outside the U.S. in London, Paris, Rome, or elsewhere.

Even when contact is initiated by phone, most journalists will request to see something in writing. They need to show the story idea to an editor, producer, or publisher and gain permission before acting.

This is best accomplished by an email—still the primary vehicle to introduce a company and story idea.

While the intent of the email is to get inside the proverbial door, the email headline provides the knock that gets the door unlocked. Editors and writers get dozens of email pitches daily. Most are quickly scanned to see if the proposed story is a good fit. The best with properly created and targeted subject lines gets read.

Many do not, even though the story itself may have some value.

Publications with the highest readership and most authority receive the most pitches. In this highly competitive scenario, correctly crafting the subject line helps to rise above the noise. The same holds true for network news and key industry trade journals. An engaging subject line also produces an uptick in local and regional coverage.

PR professionals learn that the more intriguing the email subject line, the more likely a journalist will read the body of the message. Once they reach that point—provided your story is engaging and on point—the odds of coverage tilt in your favor. Mastering the art of compelling subject lines comes down to five key elements:

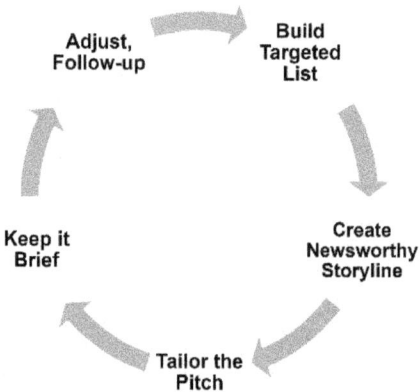

1. Target the Right Reporters and Editors

The perfect throw means nothing if the dart doesn't hit the target. The first step is to send the email to the right person—the one who covers the industry and niche served by your business and client. This can be found by researching targeted publications and writers. Pay attention to specific writers and the industry segment they cover. This prevents sending a pitch about new cookware to a writer who covers the banking industry.

Similarly, a journalist may cover new restaurant openings but not new food products and gadgets. Updated lists of journalists and emails can be purchased from a variety of sources. They can be well worth the investment, saving time and often frustration.

2. **Create a Newsworthy Subject Line**

This is the most important part of the pitch. Without a newsworthy subject line, you run the risk of your email getting buried in a crowded inbox. I have seen attention grabbing parts of a news item buried in the body of the email. It's similar to a treasure chest mired on the bottom of the ocean, requiring a lot of effort to reap the rewards. The subject line should be like a headline in a newspaper. It should have enough news value to elicit continued reading and interest.

3. **Tailor it to the Medium**

The email subject line should differ depending on your target. A television producer requires visuals—think not only telling but showing. The more visual the subject matter, the better. As a practice I will often include "good visuals" in the subject line to capture their interest.

A print reporter may be interested not only in the news you are pitching, but also the back story—the history of the people who helped the company succeed. They have room to go into depth, so be ready to support your case with hard numbers and prospects for growth.

4. **Keep it Brief**

The headline is just that—a headline. It is not the entire news release. While there is no steadfast rule on length, too many words will clutter the subject space.

If the pitch is too wordy and rambles on, chances are a reporter will delete it or it will end up in the junk file.

A good headline should be written well enough to excite the producer or writer. It should help steer them into the body of the news release for better consideration, and a better chance your news will be covered.

5. **Adjust for Follow-Up**

Reporters are busy. They may have seen your email, but after a few weeks, they have yet to respond.

I have found success by resending the email pitch a second time and tweaking the subject line.

"Thought you may have missed this" or "Making sure

you received this" along with the original subject line can move the story from the bottom of the pile to the top.

Following are actual strategic examples demonstrating how a powerful subject line can generate results.

Strategy #1: Target Community Trust and Consumer Awareness

St. Charles Veteran Needs Help After Contractor Scam—Local Businesses Step In, But More Needed

This subject line was used to pitch a story about a local veteran who paid for repair work that was never completed. My firm worked with a large, local electrical company that was part of a team of construction-related firms that wanted to help a veteran in need. The veteran lived in a mobile home, was short of funds, and had paid for repair work that had started but was never completed—leaving his home nearly unhabitable.

We crafted a pitch that brought reporters from all three local network affiliates to the veteran's home and resulted in multiple stories. Many companies stepped up and provided the veteran with the appliances and manpower needed to update the home. Our client was interviewed on camera as part of the rehab effort. Once all the repairs were completed, several TV crews came back to feature the veteran's new and improved home.

It was a win for the client, a win for the TV station, and most of all, a huge lift for the veteran.

- An empathetic twist: A veteran needs help.
- Consumer awareness: Alerting citizens to be aware of similar construction scams.
- Community trust: TV stations assist in locating companies to help a veteran get repairs.

Strategy #2: Introduce a New Local Spa with a Physician Owner and Operator

Local Hospital Physician Leaves Lucrative Practice; Opens First MD Supervised Spa in St. Louis

An effective subject line helped build branding and awareness for a local physician leaving one of the largest hospitals in the St. Louis area to start a health spa. He wanted to create a spa that combined the traditional fare—massage, nutritional counseling, and aesthetic services—with physician-supervised physicals and comprehensive medical consultations in a relaxing spa environment. He would not only own the spa but operate it.

The physician wanted to generate branding and awareness, and desired media coverage. The email subject line provided the incentive for reporters to question why a local physician would leave a thriving practice and open a health spa. A typical approach might have used a subject line of "New Spa Opens in St. Louis" but would clearly miss the compelling parts of the story. The pitch generated two TV feature stories and resulted in several features in print publications, helping position the physician in his new effort, and, at the same time, launching the brand.

- ➢ Community: Local readers will find it relevant.
- ➢ Newsworthy: A physician leaving a lucrative practice for a career change to a medically supervised spa separated this story from others.

Strategy #3: Create a Heartwarming Story About a National Woodworking Company

St. James, Missouri Company Gives Ex-Felons and Former Drug Addicts a Second Chance

A well-crafted subject line helped Cohen Woodworking attract the attention of an Associated Press reporter seeking companies supporting second-chance individuals. The owner overcame a troubled past, turning his life around. He believed he got a second chance at life and was providing the same opportunity to help others like him. The owner wanted to offer them a chance of community and purpose.

Once the AP reporter got all the details, she thought it was a story worth telling, and she did—resulting in hundreds of placements nationwide. The same subject line was tweaked for use with St. Louis area television stations and resulted in two long feature stories on the CBS and NBC affiliates. This resulted in a ten-fold increase in web traffic, Facebook activity, and more.

- ➢ Hook: Heartwarming story pulls at emotions.
- ➢ Community: Local relevance for the business owner.
- ➢ Newsworthy: Positive framing for opportunity and redemption.
- ➢ Targeted Media: Locating a reporter(s) interested in companies with second-chance employees; other reporters without that interest wouldn't provide the coverage.

In a career that has spanned over three decades, I have made hundreds of story pitches. Many have resulted in immediate coverage—or depending on timeliness and importance—have resulted in a client story within weeks or months of the initial email.

The road to success begins with a well-crafted and impactful storyline.

The challenge for the PR professional is to craft a subject line sharp enough to cut through the digital clutter—one that sparks interest, gains attention, and unlocks your story. Master the subject line, and you'll land the coverage.

TOOLBOX TAKEAWAYS

- The properly crafted subject line increases the opportunity the email will be read by journalists.
- The subject line should read like a newspaper headline, brief as possible and enticing the recipient to learn more.
- Subject lines and emails should be tailored to the medium.
- Crafting a solid email improves coverage and results.

25
Measuring What Matters

You've just spent tens of thousands of dollars on a public relations campaign—so how do you know if it's working?

Measuring the effectiveness of a campaign can be subjective depending on whom you ask. It is often viewed through the eyes of the beholder. It's discussed. Debated. Yet, it remains universally undefined.

Some say: "Audience reach. Sentiment. Share of voice."

Others argue: "Advertising value equivalency. Social echo. Messaging conveyance. Elevated search."

A few reply: "Click-throughs. Web hits."

No matter how it's defined, measurement isn't just about tracking numbers—it's understanding what those numbers mean. And interpreting those numbers depends on the resources at hand.

Those working with large corporations will have a larger array of Key Performance Indicators (KPIs), and metrics at their disposal. Smaller firms not so much.

The end game, though, remains basically the same.

Create a campaign that delivers the results your client wants. Accomplish it with a return on investment that far exceeds its costs. Media relations pros must demonstrate that the coverage generated directly boosts brand awareness and strengthens positioning—and ultimately drives revenue and enhances valuation.

Many in the industry have invested time, even careers, to demystify the measurement process.

> ➢ Katie Delahaye Paine, a pioneer in the field of communication measurement, has founded three companies (KDPaine & Partners Inc., The Delahaye Group, and Paine Publishing) dedicated to public relations measuring and consulting.

- Muck Rack is a PR software company that offers a variety of tools and formulas to help document and improve campaign results.
- Michael Smart, a top PR thought leader, operates the Inner Circle of public relations professionals. He offers tips and advice for highlighting successes in line with corporate goals.

I have found that the most effective measurement tools depend on the goals of the business and the vision of the CEO or business owner. Articles and TV coverage will drive traffic to the company's website and social media pages—but will it change sentiment, differentiate the business from its competitors, convey new messaging, or influence behavior?

A "measuring stick," an apparatus to measure the differences generated by the campaign as opposed to periods of inactivity, is necessary to calculate the resulting action.

For many seeking more online activity, this includes measurement beyond web hits. Think newsletter signups, white paper downloads, reservations at a hotel or restaurant, forms for inquiries on product sales, the number of phone calls for more information, and other forms of engagement.

The CEO and/or marketing team should have mechanisms in place to deal with an uptick in traffic and the online tools in place to create the desired action.

For more accurate results, PR professionals should have access to relevant sales data to establish a baseline—comparing standard levels of customer acquisition with the impact generated by the campaign.

Data should reflect more than a single sales order; it should also reflect potential lifetime value, which is essential in measuring a campaign's true impact. For example, a bundled streaming service campaign may gain a new customer, generating $500 annually in immediate revenue. Over the next 10 years, that same customer could continue subscribing, bringing their lifetime value to $5,000 in total. When measuring the campaign's impact, one must account for the lifetime value rather than solely focusing on the initial sale.

Not all impact comes with a dollar sign. Many forms of measurement have value:

Audience Reach

Your message is only as powerful as the audience it reaches. Proper targeting is key, with measurement based not only on total viewers or readers, but on the demographics that matter most.

Should your feature appear on the 10 p.m. local news on two different outlets—one with an average audience of 100,000 and the other with 80,000—the story could have been seen by 180,000 people.

Those numbers can be broken down to highlight the potential viewers in different demographics, aligned with the business's targeted audience, such as women 25-54 or men 18-34. Understanding which demographics are the most engaged allows the messaging to be tailored for maximum impact. Audience reach isn't just a number—it measures the influence of a campaign and ensures the right audience is reached, not just the largest.

Social Media Engagement

Social media provides the ripple effect-content surging through different channels. The echo brings your message to life in different ways. It can amplify a story on traditional media and bring it to thousands more.

Links are often shared on multiple platforms by the media and others. Many originate with a local television station or newspaper and get syndicated on national outlets like MSN or Yahoo News. Compelling stories travel fast, getting shared and reposted by team members and their connections.

Numbers will showcase how many people viewed it, engaged with it, or mentioned it. It will also quantify how many people replied or responded directly to your social pages as a result of the coverage.

Share of Voice

Exclusive features. Domination of industry trends articles. Lead exposure on a topical TV news story.

Share of voice (SOV) is sometimes overlooked as an indicator of campaign effectiveness. Yet it is a good barometer of how a brand stacks up against its competitors. It details how many earned media stories and mentions a brand receives in a selected time period as opposed to others in the same category.

A luxury hotel constantly generating feature stories and favorable reviews during the busy travel season will gain a foothold versus other operators. The same holds true for restaurants and retailers, and those in the business-to-business arena who target key industry trade journals.

Many assign a point scale to story placements. A large feature article where no other competitors are discussed receives a very high score. One where the company is mentioned along with several other competitors would receive a lower grade.

Quality of placement should also be considered. An article or sizeable mention in the New York Times or The Wall Street Journal would normally have greater value than one in a local business publication.

Key messaging communication should also be given priority. Quotes from a CEO imparting company branding, culture, and upward trajectory should generate a high score no matter the publication.

Companies and brands can determine the right methodology to score SOV and how to apply it for future efforts. It helps to size up a brand against its competitors and, if necessary, adjust for better results.

Content Worthiness

Great stories generate great content. Many media placements can be "measured" for how they translate for use within a company's full branding arsenal. Some earned media will result in top tier placements in highly regarded publications. These build not only awareness but high levels of trust and influence. They can be used and repackaged for the company newsletter, on blogs, and on social platforms.

Top-tier placements can be posted on the corporate website, used as a sales tool, and by HR as part of the recruiting process. These types of features have high value not just for the brand, but for company reputation. Many provide a high level of credibility that can be shared with clients, potential customers, and stakeholders for months, years, and even decades.

I have worked with dozens of clients with varying degrees of expectations and measurement criteria. Some were not only interested in the campaign results, but also the time spent working on each individual placement—not just in hours, but in ten-minute intervals.

Others were more interested in a consistent branding approach without regards to a time element. They were enthused with a regular flow of media exposure on a monthly basis. Then there are those business owners who simply enjoyed seeing themselves highlighted in the media.

No matter the criteria, the PR professional must secure clear alignment on expectations with the client, marketing director, or agency manager. Targeted metrics can be crafted to meet each specific need.

While there is no universal standard for measurement, PR pros can document that while metrics matter—there's much value beyond the measuring stick.

TOOLBOX TAKEAWAYS

- Many methods of measurement can be utilized to determine the effectiveness of a PR campaign.
- While some are put into practice, and some are not, brands and agencies should agree on how to place proper value on each metric.
- The goal is to demonstrate improvements in brand awareness and positioning-and ultimately impact revenue and valuation.

26
PR Drives Value and Brand Equity

Brands need to fight to be heard. Posts on social media are here one minute, gone the next. TV stories appear on one newscast then disappear for breaking or other news. Newspaper articles become the topic of the day, then get archived.

To be heard and remembered, a brand needs to break through the clutter. The proper use of PR is an art that not only elevates a brand but increases company value.

Public relations is a long game that not only enhances the overall "branding experience" but can have an impact on whether the company is able to reach its full long-term potential.

A PR campaign helps individuals dig deeper and learn more about the company values and culture. It goes beyond the surface, much like buying a new car. You go beyond the flashy exterior, look under the hood, and kick the tires to understand what drives it. That's what PR does for a brand.

When a company operates successfully and is backed by a strong, recognizable brand—it becomes more valuable than a business with little or no brand recognition.

Why?

Brands establish an emotional bond with the customer. Buyers choose brands based on perceived value and their own experience. Customers prefer brands they know such as Apple, BMW, Campbells, Coca-Cola, Hallmark, Tide, and Starbucks. The brand equity of these companies adds a multiplier 2x or more to book value. The same can hold true for your business, no matter what niche you are in.

So, what is a brand?
It's not a logo, an ad, or a sales piece.

Jeff Bezos, the founder of Amazon, said, "Your brand is what people say about you when you are not in the room." He implied the importance of reputation in shaping a brand. It suggests that a brand's true value lies in the perceptions and conversations of others, rather than solely in marketing efforts or controlled messaging.

The brand becomes a customer's entire experience in purchasing products from your company as opposed to doing business with someone else. The promise you make to deliver the highest quality product possible, in a respectable time period, and at a fair price. Think about the top brands. They excel at every phase of product creation, perception and delivery.

A good example is *Kantar BrandZ's 2025 Most Valuable Global Brands Report*, highlighting the best of the best. It measures brand equity around the world, ranking the world's leading brands based upon their financial performance, marketing innovation, and consumer perceptions. They researched the opinions of 4.5 million respondents about 22,000 brands across 538 categories worldwide, and identified the top 5 most valuable brands:

Apple, $1.3 trillion
Google, $944 billion
Microsoft, $885 billion
Amazon, $886 billion
Nvidia, $509 billion

These brands have built powerful connections, allowing them to create shareholder value faster, resist market downturns, and recover sooner from recessions.

A reliable brand's most fundamental role is a shortcut on decision making. Purchasers know what they are getting and its related value every time they buy a product, whether it be a Coke, Kleenex tissue or Tide detergent.

PR can help create that value by building authenticity, generating leadership positioning, improving relationships with stakeholders, changing perceptions and behavior, and facilitating a call to action.

Building a top brand has many advantages.
- Builds a sustainable competitive advantage
- Boosts revenue growth by increasing demand and market share
- Improves margins with premium pricing and better supplier terms

> Reduces capital requirements by minimizing the costs into new categories
> Sets the company apart by overcoming commoditization and reducing risk

Branded companies, well known in their targeted trade areas, can often charge a little more for their products and services. Customers know what they are going to get. There is no guess work.

So how do you ascertain whether a brand is strong or weak?

Salespeople are a good source for this type of information. When they visit prospective customers, they can solicit feedback as to why the prospect chose the current vendor they use. Salespeople can find out why their company wasn't contacted to submit a bid or merit strong consideration to land the business.

And they can learn what the current prospect knows about the firm (perception, if they have any at all). The targeted buyer may elicit some feedback that can reveal insights about how the company is perceived.

Customer Feedback

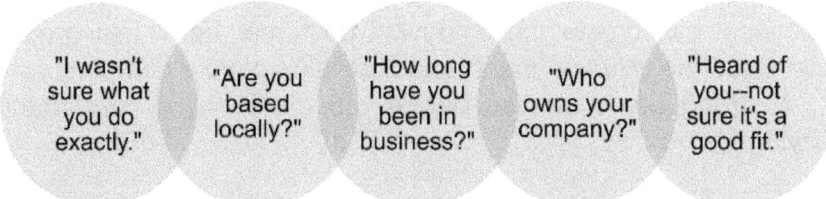

If the salesperson hears these responses, then your branding needs some work.

Is the brand built to last or does it fade into the crowd? A strong brand speaks before you do.

Signage on a major road or highway is a good indicator of strong brands that automatically connect with the customer. Think Lowes, McDonalds, Target, and Walmart. They have established value and brand equity. The sign says it all, one needs no explanation.

One way to determine if the brand has any strength is to invite customers and prospects to a focus group or two and discover what those people think and "feel" about the company.

Share of voice will reveal a lot about the brand. When people think of products in the industry, who do they think of? Do the newspaper and business publications come to you for stories and quotes or do they go to your competitors?

If the brand isn't typically part of the conversation, the brand isn't part of the decision.

Finally, the sales report can indicate if the brand is strong or weak. Flat or declining sales over the last several years can indicate the lack of a strong brand, the need to reinvigorate your campaign—or both. An upward sales curve indicates your message is getting through and you have brand strength.

Should your brand have gotten a little stale there are ways to rekindle the flame. Analyze your PR approach and assess your marketing materials and logos for relevancy and modern appeal. Do research to ascertain how the brand is perceived by the community. Develop a plan that reaches your target audience.

Remember your brand is not just a logo or website but an entire experience a customer associates with the company. The company brand is your most valuable asset. The right blend of company performance, and ongoing marketing and public relations, can create the emotional customer bond that greatly increases the value of your brand and value of your company.

A strong brand speaks before you do. What is your brand saying?

TOOLBOX TAKEAWAYS

- PR helps increase brand value and company equity.
- Highly branded companies have greater book value than unknown firms.
- Public relations creates competitive advantage, higher perceived quality, and the ability to charge more.

27
Agency Lifeblood: Winning New Clients

Connection. Reputation. Expertise. A PR firm's survival depends on attracting new clients. It is the lifeblood of any agency. Why?

Growing a client base is essential to long-term profitability. New business wins provide the infusion to overcome losses accrued through a fast-paced cycle of client mergers, acquisitions, ownership change, and new management seeking a different approach.

Winning new clients though is more than just metrics, goals, or revenue. Think of it in terms of your own reputation, your own PR campaign. These campaigns don't always speak for themselves, but your current clients do.

Someone once said, "In business, it's not only who you know, but who knows you."

Networking and visibility are key. Whether you belong to groups that meet in-person or online, the ability to offer your expertise and develop new connections will help the agency thrive.

Our agency has benefitted from many referrals—gaining an entry into the Anthony Robbins organization, connections with the owner of Amini's Home Rugs and Game Room, opened doors at a local hospital, and more. Each became a sizeable account with solid relationships, and a win-win for both their business and our agency.

Opportunities to acquire new clients also come through searches and an online presence. An agency must maintain visibility across the right channels—whether through social media such as LinkedIn, niche or trade group sites, or a significant category listing on Google, Bing, and other search engines.

It begins by establishing the agency's own public relations campaign. The ideal client and value proposition must be defined.

What is the client's problem and what solution can you provide?

How can you differentiate your firm and your expertise from other similarly perceived agencies?

Consider industry focus.

Firms specializing in a particular sector like technology, healthcare, or fashion can develop deep industry expertise. Consider targeting niche specific companies such as startups, established corporations, and those in between. Geographic reach defines the scope whether the focus is on a specific region, or a broader national or international presence. Analyzing client needs and pain points will help determine the common challenges your ideal clients face and how your PR agency can address them.

The agency can then craft a compelling value proposition—a clear, concise statement outlining the unique benefits and results clients can expect from the partnership. It goes beyond simply listing services and focuses on tangible outcomes like increased brand visibility, enhanced reputation, or measurable business growth.

Client acquisition varies based on the size and scope of the firm. Small, mid-sized, and large agencies approach the process in unique ways and each have their own set of challenges.

Small Firms

Small (boutique) PR firms often find success specializing in a specific industry or type of client. They not only build a wealth of industry expertise but position themselves as experts in a chosen field. Small firms emphasize personalized service and excel at hands-on attention with tailored strategies with direct access to senior-level professionals. They build strong relationships with journalists, influencers, and industry contacts crucial for securing media coverage and attracting new business. They are agile and can respond quickly to market trends or client needs without managerial layers, appealing to startups and mid-sized businesses.

- ➢ Rely heavily on referrals.
- ➢ Utilize content marketing to establish expertise—blog posts, case studies, thought leadership pieces.
- ➢ Participate in community events to gain visibility.

- Ensure personalized client attention.

Mid-Sized Firms

Mid-sized firms provide expanded service offerings to a wider range of clients. These can include a mix of traditional and digital PR services, crisis communications, influencer marketing, and content creation. These agencies strive to strike a balance between personalized client attention and the ability to handle a larger client base. The team is more structured than a boutique firm but still prioritizes direct client interaction. While referrals remain important, mid-sized firms also utilize targeted marketing efforts to gain new clients.

- Form partnerships with complementary businesses leading to referrals and expanded offerings.
- Expand digital marketing efforts—email marketing, SEO, and social media advertising.
- Larger budget enables investment in CRM systems, media monitoring tools, and analytics platforms to streamline operations and enhance client reporting.
- Implement targeted outreach strategies using various tools to identify and connect with potential clients.

Large Global Firms

The game plan is different for large global PR firms. Their growth strategy focuses on acquisitions to rapidly expand their geographic reach and specialized talent. These agencies utilize a wide range of client acquisition channels including email marketing, search campaigns, social media advertising, and content marketing. Larger agencies focus on building a strong brand and reputation, leveraging their global presence to attract high-profile clients.

- Structured to handle larger clients.
- Extensive networks and resources enable complex campaigns and broader audience reach.
- Invest heavily in talent acquisition with ongoing training and development.

No matter the size of the agency, the priority should be to deliver an exceptional client experience. A solid client base does more than generate a profit for an agency—it establishes credibility, strengthens the reputation, allows for sustainable growth, and expands its influence. Client retention builds lasting partnerships and attracts new business through powerful word-of-mouth referrals.

Agency personnel should be highly responsive and proactive, responding quickly to client inquiries, and providing updates and insights—keeping the client's goals and objectives at the forefront. Regular feedback from clients is more than just checking a box—it's an opportunity to exceed expectations, identify areas for improvement, and swiftly address missteps.

As the PR landscape evolves with new communication channels and strategies, successful firms can stay ahead of the curve by watching trends in industry publications, following influencers, and attending webinars and events to sharpen their edge. They can embrace new tools and platforms to streamline workflows and enhance client results. Performance metrics can be tracked to measure the effectiveness of the agency's client acquisition strategies and identify best practices.

Successful agencies develop a strong heartbeat that is honed and conditioned for the long term. Like a fine-tuned athlete they create peak performance with a process that builds credibility, expertise, and a strong value proposition in-line with a prospect's needs. They are constantly in search of the "win", realizing new client acquisition is crucial to their survival.

TOOLBOX TAKEAWAYS

- New client acquisition is crucial to building agency sustainability.
- Agencies should create their own PR campaigns, developing strategies to build reputation and connect with targeted clients and industry niches.
- Strategic approaches and tools for growth will vary by agency size.
- Development of a robust client acquisition engine ensures a steady flow of business and future success.

28
Embrace the Future

Adapt. Adjust. Embrace the change.

The familiar is always giving way to something new. In the classrooms, typewriters became keyboards, chalkboards became white boards. And in offices, technology transformed the way we worked—from paper files to digital systems, from in-person roles to remote jobs. Change is hard to accept but is a necessary part of adapting to life.

The Early Days

Workplace culture has shifted. When I first started my career in public relations, life looked much different than it does today. The business landscape was different, too.

No internet. No cell phones. No Amazon. No e-books. No online bookstores. Media relations meant calling reporters and meeting them in person.

News releases and other materials were sent by courier or mail. Eventually, the fax machine emerged and made things easier.

The Digital Revolution

Soon the internet and email replaced the fax machine as the main form of business communication. Many veteran PR practitioners I knew weren't eager about learning all the nuances of the world wide web. They were overwhelmed—and either retired or moved on to other professions. Others envisioned the new technology as a grand opportunity. Instead of running away from the new technology, they embraced it. They learned it. They applied it to increase their value to both their agency and their clients.

Some PR professionals were a step ahead of the curve. They were able to work with clients to incorporate this new world into business messaging and communications. Many of us took classes. We read about the internet in trade journals and then experimented with it. With effort and plenty of trial and error, it soon came into focus.

The emergence of digital resources, platforms, and new applications provided more and varied opportunities for message delivery. Websites, once the centerpiece of the online positioning effort, still matter. Yet they have morphed from vast digital brochures into compact designs built for quick reading and searching, not only for laptops but also for tablets, iPads, and iPhones.

Social media has more than flexed its muscle as a communications tool. YouTube continues to grow as a dominant vehicle through ample use of video. Instagram and TikTok are favored by the younger generation and its large group of influencers. Facebook still earns a dominant place. LinkedIn is a major player for those seeking job opportunities and others wishing to generate business leads and thought leadership. X and others are aligned to offer topical news trends and the opportunity for readers to voice their opinions.

Other tools such as blogs, podcasts, and online magazines, offer additional ways to deliver messaging and establish thought leadership.

Most were trained in traditional media—newspapers, television, magazines, and radio. Though message delivery has changed, the underlying structure remains the same. Even in today's ever-evolving digital world, the core principles still apply. At the center of any campaign, defining a business objective, analyzing primary audience targets, creating messaging, and selecting proper communication channels all hold—no matter the type of campaign.

Artificial Intelligence (AI)

Today, AI is changing the game, impacting not only the public relations industry—but all businesses. Chat GPT, Microsoft Copilot, and other software applications can generate news releases and other written materials in a matter of seconds.

Rules can be created to enable the software to create sample headlines and potential email pitches to journalists. Topical articles and ad copy can be developed, as well as content for social media posting.

As of this writing, the end-product created by AI must still be reviewed, edited, and nuanced for use by the specific business or client. Though not perfect, AI provides vast time savings and can make the job of the public relations professional more efficient. Some repetitive tasks such as media monitoring, data analysis, and content creation can all be automated.

The hours saved can be used to work on other clients' needs and agency responsibilities.

AI will no doubt play a greater role in the months and years ahead. Those concerned about how the technology will affect their jobs should not flee from its use but rather grasp all its benefits. Much like the advent of the internet and cell phone, PR pros should follow the leads of veterans who have thrived despite multiple changes in communications delivery. Younger professionals wishing to make their mark and rise within their business or agency should develop a leading-edge mindset.

Evolving with Technology

Learn, experiment, test all the variables AI can offer, as well as the digital platforms and resources that empower the PR professional. Enroll in training programs, classes, and webinars. Create conversations with industry thought leaders. Build a strong inner foundation. New insights can be passed on to other agency members and shared with clients.

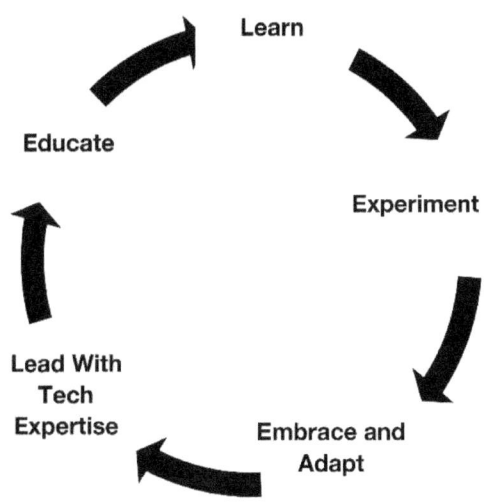

Strive to be the go-to expert for both AI tools and digital resources in your business or agency. Stay up to date on trends and new technologies as they occur. Those who seize the opportunity to learn and grow will be of high value, and on the precipice of a long and successful career.

The end result elevates the PR professional to expert status not only in the eyes of their manager, but also the clientele the agency serves. Change is constant in the practice of public relations. Embrace that, and you, the PR professional, will not only survive amidst ever-changing technology—but thrive.

TOOLBOX TAKEAWAYS

- PR is constantly evolving, and it has become crucial to learn and grasp new technologies.
- Public relations professionals on an upward career trajectory should take classes and webinars to grasp AI and new innovations. They can become an AI thought leader within their business or agency.
- To thrive, industry practitioners should not run away from the future but embrace it.

Part II
Campaigns That Work

Campaigns bring your message to life. This is where everything comes together—the highlighted strategies, skills, and insights in real-world scenarios. What follows are campaigns from Solomon/Turner demonstrating how the principles of PR translate into results.

Campaign #1
The Million Dollar Baseball

This campaign knocked it out of the park.

Public Relations professionals often become front and center, steering a major news event in the eye of a media storm. In this case, the turbulence would not be caused by heavy winds, rain, and floods, but rather the deluge of batted balls lofted majestically into the far reaches of a baseball stadium.

In 1998, the mighty gusts would find their way into St. Louis in the form of the Major League Baseball home run race. A showdown for the ages to break Roger Maris' long standing record of 61 home runs in a single season. A former New York Yankee, Maris had set the record in 1961.

It had stood for 36 years. No one thought it would ever be broken.

Up to the plate stepped two players from two rival teams. Mark "Big Mac" McGwire of the St. Louis Cardinals—a giant hulk of a man standing 6 feet five inches—against the more compact but muscular Sammy Sosa of the Chicago Cubs.

That summer, the two become lock-stepped in the home run chase of a lifetime. By early September, McGwire had 60 four-baggers to his credit and Sosa had 55.

It appeared more a question of *when* than *if* the record would be broken.

The story's prominence took it beyond the sports pages. In many cases, it was front page news and featured on network newscasts.

A sports memorabilia company in Chicago wanted to get in on the action. Their goal was to get on the map and become nationally known. The firm put their resources together and decided to offer $1 million to the person who caught the ball that broke the record.

The next step was to let the world know about it.

Through a mutual contact, the Chicago company contacted us for ideas and engagement. They wanted to build their brand with the Chicago media, and potentially nationwide. The firm realized hundreds of media outlets would likely be onsite for an upcoming Cubs-Cardinals showdown, with the homerun record on the line.

We agreed on a deal and a strategy.

Strategy

With little time to prepare we needed to step into the batter's box to deal with this 100 mile PR fastball coming right at us. The best plan was to hold a news conference.

The client was able to rent a large room in a hotel close to the stadium. Preparations started to unfold. The Cubs and Cards series was set to begin September 7. If McGwire did not break the mark beforehand, we knew the city would be filled with journalists from all over the country. Dozens would be covering it much like a World Series.

As a former sports reporter who covered baseball, pennant races, and more, I knew the routine of the media. Most have time to kill before going to the stadium.

McGwire had smashed his 61st home run the day before, in the first game of the series. The second game of the series would be played the next night. We put together the press conference for mid-afternoon several hours before game #2.

In addition to the million dollar reveal, we had a jumbo-sized ceremonial check to present to the fan that caught the home run ball. It would serve as a nice visual piece for photographers.

To make the event ever more appealing, my partner came up with the idea of a baseball fashion show showcasing our client's collection of vintage jerseys once worn by a variety of Major League players. We contacted local high schools and asked several to send over their best baseball players to be our models. The players had a chance to wear a cool jersey, walk down the aisle, and perhaps be on local and national television. Nearly everyone accepted.

Our firm made sure all the writers and TV reporters knew about the event. In addition to the standard practice of sending out news releases and making some phone calls, we took news alerts down to the ballpark area where the journalists would be congregating and handed them out. Everything came together.

Dozens of journalists attended. The story made the early

newscasts on national and local television. I even held the ceremonial check as our client hosted the news conference and took questions from the media.

Should McGwire break the record that night, the story would surely be in nearly every newspaper in America the next day. Our client was positioned to receive millions of dollars more of earned media coverage.

That is, until the unexpected happened.

On cue that evening, McGwire indeed hit homerun number 62. The ball was hit into the lower area near the bullpen, just over the left field wall. As is customary in baseball, the game came to a halt. TV crews ascended onto the field. McGwire made a few comments on the PA system.

Everyone's attention then turned to the ball. Where was it? Who had this special piece of baseball history?

Entering from the left field area was a red-clad young man. He approached the field, accompanied by security guards.

He was a member of the Cardinal's grounds crew, one of a small group who attends to the landscaping of the playing surface.

As he neared the center of the field, he clutched this special baseball. A once in a lifetime prize that could pay for college expenses, a down payment on a house, or a new car.

The young man approached the Cardinal slugger. He then unselfishly placed the ball into the hand of the man who hit it.

There would be no seven figure pay day. No more interviews for our client. Our story was over. Almost.

Impact

The process was still a win. The news conference yielded hundreds of thousands of dollars of earned media for the client. We opened doors for his business with writers who covered the sports memorabilia beat such as USA Today.

This would benefit him for future stories.

It also enhanced the client's reputation with the local Chicago media, laying the groundwork for more regional coverage in the future. Our client was greatly satisfied, and so were we—proving we could dive into a media storm, create a top-flight event, and deliver a few public relations home runs of our own.

CAMPAIGN TAKEAWAYS

- **Demonstrate Creativity, Flexibility, and Community Impact**
  The fashion show added to the event, not only helping showcase some of the client's rare jerseys but highlighting local schools and their baseball teams as It well.
- **Maximize the PR Value of an Event**
  It wasn't just about the million dollar baseball, it ignited a discussion for sports memorabilia where the client was in the spotlight.
- **Fish Where the Fish Are Biting**
  The national and local media were already in the city. No need for a lot of cold pitching. It just took someone to point them in the right direction and get them to the event. This can be applied to other media relations efforts.
- **Set Expectations and Anticipate the Unexpected**
  There was no certainty McGwire would hit the 62nd home run that night and when he did everyone was surprised the member of the grounds crew handed the ball back to him. We adjusted the program accordingly.

Campaign #2
Spotlighting an Icon: The Original Jeeps

The Jeep..."America's greatest contribution to modern warfare."
-- George C. Marshall, the U.S. Army Chief of Staff.

The history of the Jeep is a story worth telling. From battlefields to off-road weekending to today's family haulers, the vehicle has an extremely rich history. An American icon that has survived for over 80 years.

I never owned a Jeep and didn't know much about its origins. I knew they were fun to drive and perfect for camping and fishing, but my knowledge stopped there.

That all changed with our own off-road Jeep adventure. Publisher Max Freedman invited us to pitch a PR proposal for the book *The Original Jeeps*—a book detailing how the first Jeep was created for World War II.

Freedman had teamed with author Paul Bruno. They wanted to let the world know how the Jeep came into reality. A race against time to design, refine, and roll it off the line in less than two months—an impossibility today.

The manufacturing of the vehicle was needed to take on the fast-moving Nazi blitzkrieg, a strategic WWII attack used by the Germans that relied on speed and the element of surprise.

Yet the real tale wasn't just about the vehicles, but about the grit and resilience of the government officials, military personnel, and car companies—all coming together to forge the road ahead and create what would become the Jeep.

The book was a tribute to American ingenuity at its finest, capturing how innovation shaped a legendary vehicle.

Bruno had already begun exploring the Jeep's historical past in his book, *Project Management In History: The First Jeep,* driven by his career as a project manager and his long-time interest as a student of Jeep history.

The book was well received and generated a nice following in the trade. This new book would present a different take, written to bring the story to a wider audience.

We put a proposal together featuring case studies of authors we had worked for, complete with photos of book covers. Freedman was impressed with the prior work. The price point was agreeable, and after a review, we were awarded the business.

Freedman said we were far and away the best choice of several who pitched for the business.

We put the campaign into overdrive.

Jeep owners are an enthusiastic and tight-knit tribe, bound by a shared spirit of adventure and a legacy rooted in wartime history. If you own a Jeep, you understand. Once you purchase a Jeep, you belong to a club of adventurers and gear heads ceaselessly looking to enhance the ride and off-road experience.

Yet even without the keys to a Jeep, its spirit goes beyond ownership—embodying both its battlefield utility and enduring values of freedom, grit, adventure, and community. It's a mindset embraced by those not only behind the wheel but anyone traveling alongside.

The passionate community of Jeep owners has spawned dozens of related sites on Facebook. Literally hundreds of thousands of jeepers and wheelers peruse these pages for inspiration, meet ups, and information. Jeepers swap mechanical advice, modification tutorials, and endorse products to their peers.

Driving awareness of the book among Jeep owners on Facebook would be a key part of our strategy.

As we dug deeper into the Jeep story, we found many podcasts specifically targeted Jeep owners and automotive enthusiasts. This was ideal for reaching the primary audience. Many of the hosts made a strong push on social media to promote the interviews—an additional PR benefit. These ranged from Amazon Music and Apple Podcasts to Buzzsprout, iHeart, SOFREP, Spreaker, and more.

The Jeep's legacy, and its World War II roots, also offered a compelling story to history enthusiasts. Bruno's book brings to life the Jeep's powerful beginnings—born in wartime, built to last, and a lasting symbol of freedom. We identified numerous podcasts and online publications that were focused on WWII history, providing another strong target point.

Strategy

Equipped with the history and heart of the Jeep's WWII origins, we crafted a campaign that embraced the legacy of innovation and the off-road need for adventure. It was the opportunity to share the untold rugged beginnings of the Jeep story to those who live the Jeep life. Specific strategies included a high-impact and widespread media relations effort. The campaign focus areas included:

- Targeted markets where the Jeep had strong significance such at its current manufacturing plant in Toledo, Ohio and the birthplace of the first Jeep, the Bantam plant, in Butler, Pennsylvania.
- Jeep bloggers, book reviewers, and online writers.
- Podcasts and radio interviews. As highlighted in Chapter 15, *Podcast Power*, Bruno had previously hosted his own podcast and could discuss the subject in depth—using humor to keep the listener engaged.
- Social media including The Original Jeeps' own Facebook page as well as promoting the book on dozens of Facebook groups involving authors and Jeep owners.
- Leveraging articles and interviews for additional exposure. Any media hit would be linked and highlighted on Facebook, LinkedIn, Instagram, Twitter, etc.
- The book would be sold exclusively on Amazon and reviews would be necessary to generate credibility and relevancy.
- Any tie-in with the 80th anniversary of the iconic Jeep vehicle built in 1940.
- News releases, pitch letters and materials highlighting the book and author.

Impact

Our focused efforts to bring the rugged backstory of the Jeep to current Jeep owners and history buffs resulted in dynamic results. Launched in 2020, the campaign has generated dozens of interviews, feature articles, social postings, and increased reviews on the host Amazon site.

Though Amazon was the main hub for book sales, publicity helped spur additional placement in such outlets as Bokus, Waterstones, and other book sites across Europe. This would lead to additional news releases and coverage as *The Original Jeeps* increased its availability.

As of this writing, the book is sold in more outlets and continues to generate revenue for the publisher and author. When the Kindle version was released on Amazon, it reached a number #1 ranking in several categories.

Based on the success of the first edition of *The Original Jeeps,* a second book for those who prefer a more graphic representation was created entitled, *The Original Jeeps in Pictures.* In 2024, an updated version of *The Original Jeeps* was released on Amazon. In addition to Bantam (the original manufacturer), it includes more information and additional focus on Willys-Overland Motors and Ford's role in the creation of the Jeep.

Bruno is now recognized as one of the leading living authorities on early Jeep history and is asked to speak to groups, organizations, and museums about the vehicle and World War II related topics. A search on Bing and Google will reveal dozens of pages highlighting Bruno and the books.

The campaign continues to bridge the past and present of the Jeep—a legacy formed in wartime and continuing 85 years later. For owners, the Jeep is more than just a car, it's a way of life, representing freedom and resilience.

CAMPAIGN TAKEAWAYS

- **Analyze and Dive Deeper**
  PR pros rely on demographics, focus groups, and surveys. We dove deeper and learned about the international connected tribe of Jeep owners and enthusiasts—which was instrumental in constructing the campaign.
- **Apply the Author's Back Story**
  Bruno's expertise in project management and Jeep history helped us expand our media outreach to include outlets focused on business and manufacturing in addition to those highlighting new books, automobiles, and WW II.
- **Interviews Sell Books**
  Each time Bruno appears on radio or a podcast, a bump in book sales occurs. Audience size is a factor, but don't underestimate the power of listener interest. Small but mighty programs can make a large impact.
- **Focus on Earned Media**
  Jeep's rich history and Bruno's grand storytelling helped land dozens of interviews on radio and podcasts, and generated feature articles in newspapers and related print publication, boosting both his brand and his books.
- **Leveraging Traditional Media with Social Media**
  Stories were highlighted on all relevant social pages including dozens of Jeep Facebook groups and promotional podcast episodes—reaching thousands of additional listeners all at no charge.

Campaign #3
A Pig's Tale—One Penny at a Time

A dollar saved is a dollar earned, but a penny saved can compound into millions.

For decades children have looked forward to the magic sound of a coin gently reaching the bottom of the piggy bank. They stashed extra coins, change, and a rolled-up dollar or two into a small savings apparatus in the shape of the pig.

Everyone referred to them as piggy banks.

Many were pink and contained only one slot. Children were told to save that money for a "rainy day." The idea was to have money on hand in case of an emergency or to purchase something special.

The concept had evolved over centuries from medieval "pygg jars." Nearly everyone seemed to have a piggy bank, and its familiarity and recognizable graphic representation made it ideal to become the face of a public relations campaign.

Even in today's largely cashless world, a piggy bank is a hands-on learning tool that can still motivate kids to save and learn elementary lessons about finance that will serve them well in the future.

In fact, it formed the foundation for a corporate public relations campaign from Northwestern Mutual known as Penny The Pig.

Our client, Northwestern Mutual-St. Louis, recognized the ongoing issues of financial illiteracy. The State of Missouri had recently revised graduation requirements for students to include one-half credit of personal finance. The state instructed schools to make improving financial literacy a requirement and urged educational institutions to create classes on the topic.

Other states such as Alabama, Iowa, Mississippi, Tennessee, Utah, and Virginia also launched classes to help students learn more about money and how to prepare for their future financial needs.

In 2010, our client wanted to jump on board the financial literacy initiative.

Northwestern Mutual had created its own piggy bank, Penny. The bank was green and made of plastic. It featured four slots to demonstrate financial literacy: saving, spending, donating, and investing.

In addition to Penny the Pig banks, Northwestern Mutual developed a sister website called themint.org where students could learn tips and tricks for earning money and the value of saving. The site featured activities, challenges, and calculators for young children and teens, and advice for parents.

Strategy

I was brought in to discuss the national campaign with John Qualy, the agency's local managing partner, and Alan Robbins, a financial advisor already involved in organizations dealing with financial education.

Public relations campaigns don't happen in a vacuum. It takes buy-in from the client. Qualy and Robbins were excited and completely invested in any effort to help children become more financially literate. They supported any discussion between the student and their parents on how the child could earn and save more money.

Our goal was to create a program that inspired those discussions on a regional level.

Working as a team with Robbins and Qualy, we decided to bring the Northwestern Mutual message directly to the schools. Robbins, the father of two children, was well skilled in discussing financial related topics with kids of all ages.

Robbins said he could create a presentation designed for students and could adjust it depending on the grade level. The strategy of our efforts would then be to connect with schools across the area and secure appearances for Robbins in the classrooms.

Many area schools were immediately receptive to the idea.

Soon we were in full launch mode of the financial literacy tour. Robbins started with elementary schools and spoke to young children. His talk began with a magic trick to capture their interest.

"There's no magic to savings," he said. "You have to practice over and over again until you get it right."

The presentation then focused on needs vs wants and how far

someone should drive to save money on an item like an iPod, factoring in the price of gas. It then shifted to compounding interest and how money grows as a result.

What can a single penny do?

To demonstrate, the class was divided into two groups. In one group each student received a hypothetical sum of $5 million. In the other, each student received one penny, to be compounded and doubled in value every day.

"At the end of 31 days which would be worth more?" he asked the class.

Most were happy to receive the $5 million. Conversely, Robbins explained that if the penny doubled every day—1 cent becomes 2 cents, then 4 cents, then 8 cents, and so on—by day 31, the students who started with a single penny would have a treasure of $10 million.

While it is unlikely that a sum of money can double in value each day, the presentation demonstrated to the kids that small actions repeated over time can lead to big results.

Toward the end, Robbins would give each student a Penny The Pig bank and explain how they could use the four slots to not only help themselves but to help others.

Impact

As word about the presentation began to spread, more and more schools began to contact Robbins and us. They included both public and private schools at all grade levels. The messaging and communication of the Penny The Pig campaign was sparking a high level of interest.

One that provided learning and empowerment for hundreds of kids to take control of their money.

We invited reporters to attend several of the events. Articles in the St. Louis Post-Dispatch and Suburban Journals drove more inquiries from area educational facilities. The campaign reached over 1,000 students. While focused only on the St. Louis region, in the end, the state of Missouri ranked in the top 10 nationwide for financial education. The piggy banks proved to be much more than just empty gifts—they were the student's ticket to financial education.

Though not its intent, the campaign did more than educate kids in school. It sparked interest in the field of finance. Many students asked Robbins how they could get a job not only with an investment firm but with Northwestern Mutual. Demonstrating when a company launches a campaign with integrity and purpose, the impact goes beyond the original mission.

Robbins is a member of the Financial Planning Association and would become its local president. He remains active with multiple organizations, continuing his quest to educate young people about financial literacy. The campaign demonstrated that even the smallest sum, invested correctly, can impact lives, benefit others, and ignite a journey to financial freedom—starting with the power of just one penny.

> **CAMPAIGN TAKEAWAYS**
>
> ➢ **Locate a Company Campaign Evangelist**
> Finding an internal evangelist is key to driving maximum results. Northwestern's buy-in and full support, along with Robbin's commitment, made the effort a complete success.
>
> ➢ **Maximize Word-of-Mouth**
> Word spread to other teachers after one teacher shared details about the presentation. We leveraged these conversations to connect with more teachers and school boards, building the demand for the program and the brand.
>
> ➢ **Tell *and* Show**
> The *Penny The Pig* piggy bank was the key to the presentation—fun, hands-on, and easy for children to understand. It transformed a talk into an engaging experience.

Campaign #4
Dialing Up: An Underdog Story

In PR no two days are the same-and neither are the campaigns. Part puzzle. Part performance. A PR firm is challenged with making the impossible seem possible, the bizarre seem standard.

One such case involved a regional telecommunication startup, Birch Telecom. We were invited to pitch for the account. During the discovery interview we always ask the same question:

"Who do you envision as your competition?"

The marketing director said, "AT&T-Southwestern Bell."

At the time, AT&T was one of the largest telecommunications companies in the world. A virtual monopoly that controlled a vast amount of local and long-distance calling in the United States. It operated through a number of Bell subsidiaries in a number of markets. In the St. Louis region, it was known as Southwestern Bell.

Birch was founded in Kansas City. It had come to exist when congress passed the Telecommunications Act in the late 1990s. Politicians wanted to create competition in the telecom industry, and removed regulatory barriers for entry into any communications market. They enabled companies like Birch to enter the communications landscape as a competitive local exchange carrier or CLEC—small companies could now offer phone services and get a piece of the telecom action.

Nearly all phone services were conducted over copper wiring, and over the years, AT&T had built and owned just about all the copper wiring that supplied home telephone service in their markets nationwide. The division imposed by the government required AT&T to provide access to other companies on those same lines. Strangely, a company like Birch could rent those lines and offer telephone services at a lower price, and still make a profit.

I remember thinking, "Whoa—you're going against a multi-billion dollar conglomerate. One that could crush you at any time. Birch better have a really good story."

We formulated and pitched several ideas and were chosen against other competing agencies.

Strategy: David vs Goliath

Our charge would be to help build Birch's brand in the St. Louis region, and as a result, generate more customers. All of whom would need convincing to switch from the only company they ever knew, Southwestern Bell.

Birch analyzed that conglomerates could raise prices as necessary. Customer service can get spotty, and problems are addressed on their schedule—not yours. For a long period, there was no alternative. You got your phone bill. You paid it.

To combat the monolith, they created a message that positioned them as most smaller companies would against a giant. Smaller but faster. Flexible not rigid. Fun not stodgy.

"We are the anti-telephone company."

In true David vs Goliath fashion, they offered more efficiency and aspired to be more customer friendly. The PR campaign would highlight that messaging.

Media Relations

Since Birch was a relative unknown in the St. Louis market, media relations would play a strong role in the campaign. It focused on two areas: the business audience and individual consumers.

Earned media would be targeted at business and consumer publications. In the late 1990s and early 2000s, newspapers and magazines were in abundance and profitable. Television and radio would also play a factor. Social media was not yet relevant.

Reporters were anxious to write about this new type of telephone company. Our firm was able to secure a variety of feature articles in the St. Louis Business Journal, St. Louis Post-Dispatch, Suburban Journals, Small Business Monthly, and several others.

Radio interviews discussing any telephone related issue were also secured.

Special Events

Birch's marketing department was as flexible as their service. They were open to ideas that were fresh and could help establish their local brand. Birch did not shy away for staging a special event to positively impact the community and at the same time establish their name.

One that stood out we co-created was called "The Santa Hotline," a great fit for a telecom company.

Birch invited everyone to call a special number and they could talk to Santa "live" and give him their Christmas wish list. Parents and children were invited to call. Company volunteers manned the phones for a week or two before Christmas and did their best rendition of the white bearded figure. Some of the local TV stations invited us to talk about the hotline on-air. Yours truly even donned a Santa outfit to add some visual zest for the cameras.

Impact

A PR firm is often charged with breaking down unconventional ideas into relatable messages. Our focused efforts to build brand awareness and generate more customers for Birch yielded tens of thousands of dollars of earned media—proving that smart positioning can empower a smaller player to effectively compete against a modern-day Goliath.

Birch was able to gain a presence in the local market, amplify their brand, and build a loyal customer base. By focusing on the details and community outreach, Birch Telecom was able to prove that size alone doesn't define success.

CAMPAIGN TAKEAWAYS

➢ **Client Buy-In**
Seek to work with as much of an open slate as possible. In this case, Birch was open to new and novel ideas to build their brand. Few corporate parameters existed at the time.

➢ **Create Out-of-the-Box Approaches**
Dig deep for different approaches. Companies may surprise you with how much weight they will put behind the right idea if it's a good fit.

➢ **Planning the Attack**
Maintain strong campaign execution and control. Outlining, pitching, and assisting with media outreach is one aspect; helping a business execute events and strategies is another.

Campaign #5
Hanukkah, Oh Hanukkah

Special events. Most run just once.

The better ones have a lifespan of two or three years. Then there are the exceptional ones—whose impact is measured not in years, but decades.

In the late 1990s our agency was engaged by Schnucks (a large chain of supermarkets) and its real estate arm, now known as The Desco Group. We were asked to create a public Hanukkah Celebration at its shopping center, Schnucks Ladue Crossing, in St. Louis.

The shopping center's goal was to provide acknowledgement and even applaud the area's Jewish population for their ongoing support of the center. At the same time, they wished to bring additional recognition and awareness to the other businesses in the shopping center.

We had previously worked with the shopping center and its real estate division on other events. These were mainly Christmas celebrations with Santa appearances at Schnucks grocery stories. Research indicated there were very few, if any, public Hanukkah celebrations held anywhere in the nation—much less locally. The Hanukkah event would break new ground and connect with the community in a creative way.

Strategy

Hanukkah, of course, occurs in winter, when temperatures and weather conditions can be unpredictable. An indoor facility would be needed. Unfortunately, the center had no large meeting spaces. The owner of a large variety store, Spicer's, volunteered to host the event. In meetings with Schnucks personnel and the store owner, it was decided that kosher candy and candles could be given away at the event. In addition, a singer could be brought in to sing Hanukkah-related songs.

We developed a plan that included advertising with posters made and placed on the windows of the businesses in the shopping center. There would be large signage placed at both entrances to the center. An ad in the St. Louis Jewish Light newspaper would also be purchased.

Media relations would be a heavy focus. Appearances to discuss the event would be planned for area TV and radio stations. Many print publications (there was no social media of consequence at the time) had event sections and calendars that could feature photos and details.

The concentrated effort produced a nice turnout for the initial event. However, it was burdened by a lack of space due to aisle upon aisle packed with merchandise. It limited interaction between youngsters and families.

The store was designed for retail, not large gatherings.

Booking A Solution

Based on the enthusiastic turnout at Spicer's, but encumbered with the store's layout challenges, we conferred with Schnucks' personnel to move the event to a larger store, Barnes & Noble Booksellers.

The bookstore was prominently located in the shopping center on the opposite side of the street from Spicer's. In addition to books, Barnes & Noble had a dedicated area utilized for children's events. This included a stage and a few rows of bleacher seats to accommodate youngsters.

Barnes & Noble management agreed to host the next event. In addition to the bleacher seating, they said they could move some shelves and set up chairs for adults. They agreed to do whatever was necessary to ensure the event's success.

Creating A Partnership

The move to Barnes & Noble provided larger space and with it, the ability to improve the event's entertainment value. We envisioned forming a relationship with a Jewish school. The goal was to provide an opportunity for the school's choir to sing Hanukkah songs in front of an audience and gain some notoriety.

A "partnership" was created with H.F. Epstein Hebrew Academy. The school not only had its own choir, but also an educator and storyteller who could weave in a few Hanukkah stories. The school's headmaster realized the Hanukkah Celebration would not only have high PR and branding value, but would also help recruit students.

They agreed to work with us.

Their participation took the event to a new level. Their student families turned out in large numbers as did others from the community. It became a winning situation for both the school, Barnes & Noble, and the shopping center. The bond formed with Epstein has been ongoing. Though headmasters have changed, the event has survived for over two decades. In fact, many who once attended as children are now grown and married—and bring their own children to the Hanukkah Celebration. A passing of the torch from generation to generation.

Impact

A strong media relations effort had been central to the event's success. This included TV interviews prior to the event with the school's headmaster and our agency, as well as mentions on TV weather segments. It now features social media promotion on Facebook, Instagram, radio interviews, and listings in event calendars—both in print and online.

TV and print reporters have been in attendance to create stories. Several features have resulted. Post-event coverage with photos are now placed on social media and sent to print publications.

More than a "special event," the Hanukkah Celebration has become a community staple and remains the longest running celebration of its kind in the St. Louis area.

CAMPAIGN TAKEAWAYS

- **Create Client Partnerships That Are Invested in Your Campaign or Cause**
  This has been the case of the shopping center and Barnes & Noble who fully support the Hanukkah Celebration.
- **Seek Out Evangelists Who Can Boost the campaign**
  Evangelists can take the event to the next level. This has been true of H.F. Epstein Academy whose administration, teachers, students, and families are enthusiastic champions of the event.
- **Expand Media Outreach**
  Seek creative ways to promote an event, such as engaging with TV meteorologists to spotlight the happening on local weathercasts.

Campaign #6
The Law of Attraction

One event, one unexpected meeting, or new unforeseen circumstance can change the trajectory of a business or a career.

You don't often recognize the impact of an event when you are standing in it; sometimes the most important meetings are unplanned. But for some reason you become attracted to the person, the situation, the circumstance—pulled by a magical magnetic force.

In my case, I was sitting in the lobby of a news talk radio station in St. Louis. Our client was preparing to be interviewed. He ran a temporary employment agency and the topic was going to be hiring and job trends.

Out of the corner of my eye I noticed a gentleman entering the lobby. He was well dressed, in a business suit and carrying a stack of cassette tape albums—widely used at the time for music, audio books, and educational programs.

All of the cassette tapes featured a motivational speaker named Brian Tracy. Ironically, I had been listening to Tracy's cassettes for several months. He had compiled various lessons based on research from notable high achieving businesspeople, as well as politicians and scientists. It was all woven together in what he called *The Psychology of Success*.

The gentleman did a visual survey of the lobby, seeking a receptionist or someone to speak with. I reached out and introduced myself.

Confidently, the man introduced himself as Dan. I asked if Brian Tracy was coming to St. Louis. He said yes Brian would be visiting St. Louis for an upcoming seminar, and they were seeking publicity for his appearance.

I got excited. I told him about my firm and that I was a big fan.

I blasted out, "Just get me a few tickets to the event and we will promote the heck out of his appearance." We met and put together an agreement, basically a trade—PR for tickets.

Strategy

The seminar would be designed for salespeople and other business executives. Tracy had compiled an album called *The Psychology of Selling* and the program would help those in sales grow their client list and motivate them to sell more.

Tickets were sold two ways. One was through short sales meetings with companies who employed large selling teams. These mini seminars offered quick sales tips, a pitch about the Tracy program, and a "close" with a call to sign up. Companies would pay for the entire cost of the ticket or co-op half the price, so any salesperson who wished could go to the event.

The other method was promotional means through the media. While media coverage also generated ticket sales, Dan's team was still building its expertise in working with newspapers, radio and television.

I suggested we create a salesperson appreciation day in St. Louis, based around the seminar, and my participation in a group called Sales and Marketing Executives. It would support hard-working salespeople and be a nice hook for media coverage.

The *Salesperson Appreciation Day* turned out to be a good strategy. A lot of media coverage was generated. One of the best was a radio interview on KMOX, the top-rated radio station with the top-rated morning show. I was invited for a guest interview on the show, talking about selling and weaving in the Tracy seminar. It was humbling to sit next to two radio legends, Bob Hardy and Bill Wilkerson.

Overall, the event was successful. Hundreds of tickets were sold.

Impressed with the results, Dan asked me to go on the road and promote the next seminar. This time they agreed to a fee, and would also cover travel and expenses.

I didn't realize it at the time, but this PR train was embarking on a multi-city tour—and I would be its conductor, engineer and only passenger. Cincinnati would be the first stop.

I would arrive well in advance of the program date to build connections with the media. The process took about a week and entailed securing media sponsorship, arranging interviews for Tracy or one of his organizers, securing advertising deals, and coordinating additional methods of promotion. Most of the work thereafter could be done by phone. If necessary, I would return just before the seminar to assist with last-minute details and attend the event.

The seminar team needed about two months to line-up sales meetings, secure temporary help, and finalize all payments and invoices after the program. Funds were tight, and since I would only be there for about a week, they asked me to sleep on a cot in an empty storage space. I accepted and put up with whatever pains and stiffness resulted.

The effort produced another excellent crowd.

Soon I was working in multiple cities wherever the team could contract and book Tracy. One of the three partners left to pursue other opportunities, leaving Dan and his partner in charge. They each selected their own territories to host a seminar.

I was a man in motion working for both partners. Seminar stops included Boston, Chicago, Cleveland, Dallas, Houston, Miami, Orange County (CA), Philadelphia, Tampa, Toronto, and more.

Later, one of the members of the sales team left and went to work for an up-and-coming speaker named Tony Robbins. He called and said Robbins could use my help. I connected with Robbins' seminar manager.

We agreed to terms, and I was now representing Tracy and Robbins.

Impact

Those seminar promoters were a tight knit community. More promoters would hear about our expertise; we worked with them as well. For several years it was a truly enriching experience.

In addition to the financial rewards, it was enjoyable to work with like-minded, positive individuals. As Tracy and Robbins gained in popularity, it helped our agency attract new clients—many in other industries.

Tracy discusses the law of attraction on many of his recordings. Magically it brought me together with his seminar producer and created a PR seat on what would become a bullet train.

CAMPAIGN TAKEAWAYS

➢ **Develop Partnerships to Enhance the Campaign**
Seek out complementary organizations that can help advance your brand as well as theirs—creating a win-win for both. Such was the case with Salesperson Appreciation Day, the Tracy seminar and Sales and Marketing Executives.

➢ **Leverage Marketing and Advertising**
In addition to media relations, look for ways to expand your knowledge of marketing and advertising so you can extend the reach of a campaign.

➢ **Respond and React**
Maintain flexibility. Not everyone would be in position to run and go with the seminar promoters like I did. But if opportunities present themselves within your own personal parameters, don't be afraid to pursue them.

Campaign #7
Dot-com Daze

The Internet. An avalanche of newly formed tech companies. Cash, and plenty of it.

In the 1990s, a second California gold rush was underway. This time shovels weren't needed to find your fortune. This time, it was venture capital.

New technology, based on the widespread use of the Internet, was creating a siren chant for entrepreneurs to gather their wagons and head west. An abundance of riches could be found in a small area near San Jose, called Silicon Valley.

Online companies, known as dot-coms, were sprouting everywhere. Anything tech related seemed like the next big thing and companies were willing to invest.

Venture capitalists were willing to spend and spend big. They hoped to find founders with bold visions and business plans to match. The goal was to claim a piece of ownership, fuel a company until it went public, then generate a return in the millions if not billions.

The mantra was find a business. Invest in it. Grow it. Reap the rewards.

Accordingly, branding and name awareness became essential and a top priority. Dollars flowed into public relations and advertising.

Yet few had a solid plan. Launch first, figure it out later.

They were like competitive runners sprinting before they knew what the race was all about.

The media termed it the Dot-com bubble.

The competition among venture capitalists (VCs) became intense. The standing joke was someone just got $1 million for an idea written on a napkin.

When deals were struck, the next step would be to let the world know about the company and its prospects for rapid growth. The VCs required the startup to hire a public relations firm or an in-house person to assist in that effort.

The PR phones began to ring in California. Soon many would be dialing us.

California-based public relations firms with even a hint of tech expertise were in demand. They were hired to create brand awareness for the new companies. Agencies large and small started gobbling up clients.

The only problem—overwhelming demand, limited staff, and not enough personnel to build and execute campaigns.

Strategy

Our agency had been working with a St. Louis based IT firm. We understood most of the terminology, how tech worked, and how to apply it. Reading about the shortage of PR professionals, I decided to connect with a number of firms in the San Francisco and San Jose areas. I wanted to inform them of our expertise and availability in case they needed assistance.

Four agencies needed help "yesterday." Two more would soon follow. I had virtual phone meetings with each and picked up all types of assignments. The tasks included writing, setting up media tours on the east and west coasts, direct media pitches, and contact with their clients.

They all wanted us to move at dot-com speed. "Here's the plan. What can you do now to help us?"

One agency hired us to represent them with their client at a trade show in Atlanta. The boom in tech had spawned many new magazines and publications, and several key members of the targeted press were in attendance. My task was to interact with them, chat up the client, provide information, lay the groundwork for future articles—and do so at a fiber-optic pace.

Later, that agency would fly me out to San Jose for a meet and greet, and we collaborated on a few projects. At the time, we had a nice roster of our own clients, but this seemed like a very rare opportunity to expand our reach and expertise in tech.

As a partner at a small firm, I was fortunate to have the flexibility to add this type of business and didn't mind working 16-hour days. The financial rewards were also impressive.

For once in our industry, and perhaps never again, demand far outweighed supply.

Impact

This dot-com whirlwind, according to Investopedia, caused the value of U.S. tech stocks to rise on the Nasdaq exchange from under 1,000 to over 5,000 between 1995 and 2000.

The bubble became unsustainable and eventually burst in 2000, resulting in a crash that led to massive stock sell-offs. By its end, almost a third of companies that had emerged during the dot-com revolution had failed, and the stocks that survived traded well below their previous highs.

As a result, many of the California PR firms took a hit—a big one.

Some firms, caught up in the hysteria, staffed up, and in lieu of standard cash billings, took small positions of ownership with their clients. A decision they would later regret.

A few of the high-flying agencies closed. Those who survived, downsized. Others retooled and regrouped to focus on other areas of business.

Fortunately, our firm's client's list was diversified into areas besides technology. We were able to survive this public relations roller coaster ride.

The PR Bubble had burst and at least temporarily ended the gold rush. It caused many VC firms to regroup and refocus.

More attention was given to not only fast-tracking ideas into products, but problem/need solutions, operational experience, and an established business foundation.

Though not every company succeeded, the Dot-Com era did spawn innovative technologies and with it, a new ongoing demand for tech-related public relations.

CAMPAIGN TAKEAWAYS

- **Thought Leadership**
  While not our entire focus, at the time we were perceived as a PR tech thought leader. It helped land new business and demonstrated the value of continuous education within your niche.
- **Analyze Areas of Future Growth**
  Pay attention to trade journals, watch for industry trends, and anticipate growth in targeted business segments.
- **Maintain Aggressiveness**
  Develop an aggressive mindset when opportunities present themselves.
- **Focus on the Agency's Long Game**
  Build a roster of clients in different industries in case one segment encounters a downturn.

Campaign #8
A Woodworker Crafts Success

Carpenters begin quite simply—building things from scratch, crafting their skill, shaping their future with their hands.

Similarly, PR professionals work with a variety of businesses and entrepreneurs to help shape their stories and build on their success.

Many entrepreneurs are self-made. Some with limited expertise in their chosen field and a lack of financial resources. Through trial and error, they somehow succeed. There are those with exceptional "back stories." Ones that could form the basis for a great book or movie.

They built an amazing company. Employed many. Made an impact on their community.

Perhaps none of the clients we have worked with fits this profile better than Phillip Cohen. Cohen is the founder and recently retired CEO of Cohen Woodworking. A company providing commercial woodworking design and products to customers nationwide.

Located in the small town of St. James, Missouri, the business generates around $12 million per year and is now run by two of Cohen's sons. Cohen was raised in Chicago amid a difficult home life. As he reached college age, Cohen fled his troubled past—only to find himself in Kentucky, struggling with addiction to drugs and alcohol. In spite of the struggles, Cohen married a woman he met there, and moved to Tennessee to begin a new chapter of his life.

He sought treatment for his addictions and turned to woodworking. He made porch swings, birdhouses, and toy trucks from wood. Neighbors saw them and liked them. Phil started selling them. Eventually he got the chance to do some commercial woodworking. He turned his basement into a woodworking shop, working day and night alongside his wife. The thriving business would soon provide custom millwork for Walmart.

Soon after, Cohen moved his family and business to Southern Missouri, building and expanding the facility to over 55,000 square feet. Today, their clients include hospitals, airports, retail, and others from across the nation.

Cohen believed he got a second chance at life and wanted the same for anyone willing to do the work to improve their life. The company employs former drug addicts and those formerly incarcerated, helping them turn their lives around.

In 2017, Cohen was named Missouri's Small Business Person of the Year by the Small Business Administration. That year we received a call from one of the company's board members, a successful independent business consultant, and mutual connection. He asked us to meet with Phil, hear his story, and see if we could help him expand his business.

We were quickly engaged and sprang into action.

Strategy

Our goal was to build on the Small Business Person of the Year award and launch a full media relations campaign.

The focus would be on brand building, awareness generation, and an HR component to attract more potential employees.

Company growth from small origins to a large business serving clients nationwide would form the fulcrum of the campaign.

Phil's backstory, overcoming addiction and helping others seeking a second chance at life, would provide additional campaign focus.

Processes would include connecting with key trade journals, national media outlets, local/regional print media, online/digital publications, and television stations.

Impact

I quickly learned the Associated Press was doing a story on businesses providing opportunities for second-chance individuals. The AP loved Phil's story and featured it.

It was picked up by 500 publications.

Dozens of articles, awards, and TV stories would follow. Highlights included a cover story with Woodwork magazine, a publication we had pursued for over a year. There was a prestigious award from Forbes, who named Cohen Woodworking one of their Small Giants, companies who forgo fast growth to instead run a steady, high-quality business.

A long feature on the company ran on KMOV-TV, the St. Louis

CBS affiliate. It aired on a Thanksgiving evening newscast immediately after the last day's football game. It created a huge spike in social engagement with the firm.

The same held true for a feature story on the Making A Difference segment on KSDK-TV, the St. Louis NBC affiliate.

Additional earned media appeared in Woodworking Network and multiple trade journals, the *St. Louis Business Journal*, *Small Business Monthly*, *St. Louis Post-Dispatch* and other local publications.

In all, millions of impressions were created, enhancing Cohen's reputation, forging new connections, and driving business growth. In 2019 Cohen was named to the St. Louis Small Business Hall of Fame by *Small Business Monthly*.

The woodworker's story was rare as he overcame addiction and then built a prosperous eight-figure business. Designing a pathway for others to improve their lives. It provided more than enough tools to construct a highly successful campaign.

CAMPAIGN TAKEAWAYS

- **In-Depth Media Relations**
  Dig deep and seek out back stories of ownership or key staff for media opportunities.
- **A Novel Plan**
  Use the founder's background as a news hook and weave into a detailed story of current business growth.
- **Construct an Out-of-the Box Approach**
  Connect with journalists out of the usual business window to pursue potential placements.
- **Win the Oscar**
  Pursue awards, including national honors (such as the Forbes award) and leverage them for local coverage—an excellent way to enhance HR activities.

Campaign #9
Game On—From Newcomer to Market Leader

A good referral in PR opens doors—even when the key doesn't seem to fit the lock.

At a networking event in the early 2000s, I was referred to the owner of a new building under construction in Chesterfield, (St. Louis) Missouri. The owner was launching something big and needed PR guidance.

I made the appointment and soon ventured to the facility.

The building was extremely large and still under construction. Planks of wood were strewn everywhere. Men were working fastidiously to attach girders to beams. Others were searching through catalogs or performing administrative tasks.

I met with the CEO, Arash Amini, who introduced the space as the new headquarters of Amini's Home, Rugs and Game Room. Amini's had retail stores in Oklahoma City, Tulsa, and the Kansas City area. It was founded in 1975 by his father and operated as a family business, with his mother also actively involved.

The St. Louis store would be the largest in the group—54,000 square feet. It was within driving distance of the other stores, and Amini wanted a larger headquarters near a major metropolitan area with greater opportunities for growth.

Amini said the company's goal was to become the premier supplier of billiards tables, game room furniture, and accessories in the St. Louis area. He said his products were high-quality and backed by excellent service.

The target customer was higher income, ideally those who would be apt to remodel and upgrade an entire basement or outdoor living area. He said he was flexible and open to any creative idea to help him accomplish his goal. Amini admitted he had very few connections in the area and there was no name awareness or brand recognition.

I quickly realized this was going to be a project constructed unlike any other.

Similar to a break shot at the beginning of a game of pool, the PR balls would need to roll in multiple directions, drive to the rails, and find the winning pocket.

We moved quickly and presented a proposal. Amini said he wanted to speak to a few other agencies. We followed-up and Amini said he liked our approach best—a few days later we had secured the account.

Strategy

Armed with the company's desire for growth and luxury positioning, we crafted a campaign that would not only bring awareness to the company, but align with the affluent clientele Amini was after. This included:
- General branding awareness: familiarize consumers with the name Amini's.
- Build on the large store's brand and copper roof, "The Home of the Copper Dome", which could be seen by highway travelers.
- Special events to bring shoppers into the store.
- Media relations with local newspapers, TV and radio and other publications.
- Community building, formulating relationships with area organizations and nonprofits.
- Personal introductions of Arash Amini at events where high-end individuals would be in attendance.

I escorted Amini to several events and introduced him to CEOs and other influencers. Amini's arranged to have a championship billiards player travel to St. Louis and do an in-store demonstration. The woman, often seen at the time on ESPN, was a big media draw. We were able to secure many local sports anchors for stories. They brought camera crews and taped her making trick shots.

We developed an awards strategy that resulted in Amini securing the prestigious 40 Under 40 recognition in the St. Louis Business Journal. Other honors and stories leveraged his engaging presence and success as a CEO. It generated additional earned media and many personality focused features.

The strategy included promoting a "jail and bail" onsite fundraiser that helped bring executives to the store after they were "arrested" by police. It helped raise funds for the Muscular Dystrophy Association. KSDK TV, the NBC affiliate, and local MDA telethon station, covered the event.

Relationships with other nonprofits helped build the brand within the community. Amini's also provided game room equipment and gift cards to help raise funds for area charitable endeavors.

Impact

The campaign helped Amini's gain a competitive foothold in the St. Louis market. Amini's has dynamically increased revenue and become a staple in the area for game room equipment, theater seating, carpets, pinball and entertainment machines.

The store has grown and expanded its presence into outdoor patio furniture, lighting, and spas.

The PR campaign pushed the right levers and laid the carpet for future growth. The Amini's brand and its tagline "The Home of the Copper Dome" is well known throughout the area. The store has leveraged the internet to expand many of their offerings nationwide with prospects for greater expansion.

CAMPAIGN TAKEAWAYS

- **Networking**
  PR people should network to open new doors and expand their presence in their targeted communities. At the same time, building on their own networking skills to help others accomplish their goals.
- **Personality-Oriented Media Relations**
  Search for media coverage beyond the typical business articles. The personality profiles helped create a human element and still brand the company.
- **Oscar Worthy**
  Amini and his company won several awards, both locally and nationally. These awards positioned and branded the firm and laid the groundwork for future growth.
- **Impactful Events**
  Amini's sought out fun events with charities such as the "Jail and Bail" fundraiser. It not only targeted the right higher income audience, but also benefitted the community and generated TV coverage.

Campaign #10
Breaking Barriers: The Legendary Contracts of Jackie Robinson

The call came in unexpectedly. "I need help promoting a one-week blitz in St. Louis regarding baseball and Jackie Robinson—can you help with that?"

Our firm has an extensive background in sports marketing, and I have always been a big baseball fan. The caller described that he and a group of investors, including the well-known talk show host and newscaster Larry King, were involved.

They had secured the original baseball contracts signed by the late Jackie Robinson. The ones that broke Major League Baseball's color barrier.

The contracts had been verified by a company in New York and could be worth millions. The potential client was also in the process of setting up a collectibles website where items could be bought and sold, and a program on one of the cable channels.

The contracts would serve as a conduit for media coverage that promotes not only the legendary agreements but also to spotlight the prevalence of racism at the time, Robinson's career, and the new website and television program.

The caller said he was tasked to represent the group as its spokesperson. He was making a national tour of baseball stadiums to secure space and publicity regarding the contracts and upcoming show. He had just finished his media tour in Miami appearing at a Marlins' game.

St. Louis would be next.

I told him to give us 24 hours to discuss the project. We did our due diligence and found they had already received a lot of top tier media coverage in New York, where Robinson had been a member of the Brooklyn Dodgers. They also received coverage in Montreal, where Robinson played for the Dodgers' then minor league team, the Montreal Royals.

We came to an agreement and earned the business.

Once on-board, the client provided us additional information and scheduled events that we needed to build into our campaign. We were faced with the challenges of time constraints with the limited media tour in St. Louis, as well as obtaining media coverage for two high-profile happenings.

Strategy

With these challenges in mind, an all-encompassing media relations plan was created to generate a high-level of brand and awareness for the contracts, website, and future show. All earned media and related coverage would have to be condensed into a one-week period while the client was in St. Louis. This placed high stress and pressure on the agency and campaign, requiring a 24/7 effort.

Media coverage would be paramount. The client had signed an agreement with the Cardinals to throw out the first pitch at a game and display the contracts at the stadium. This would require us to execute on-field interviews and secure an interview on the team's radio network. The client also created a special event in Alton, Illinois to promote the contracts.

Photos and videos would also need to be secured and leveraged for additional branding on social media.

Our action plan included:
- TV interviews targeting all three network affiliates
- Radio interviews on the Cardinal Network flagship station, KMOX, and the major sports station 101ESPN
- Interviews on the Cardinal TV Network and Cardinal Radio Network
- Photos and videos of the client displaying the contracts at Busch Stadium
- Radio and print interviews at the appearance in Alton
- Leveraging all photos and videos taken during the events for additional branding on social media

The client had a commanding presence and personality, which added impact to the media coverage we needed. No media training was necessary. This helped in our efforts to maximize the quality of the interviews, convey messaging, and generate the necessary results.

Impact

The campaign yielded the desired results and more.

Interviews took place on all three local network TV news affiliates. One segment, on the FOX 2 morning show, ran for nearly 10 minutes. Other stories ran multiple times on each station.

A television interview was secured on the Cardinal's pregame show on its TV network, as well as an interview on the Cardinals' radio network that included 140 stations.

We gained a radio station interview on 101ESPN that ran for nearly 30 minutes and one on the KMOX morning radio show.

We also earned traditional press coverage. Print articles ran in various forms in the *St. Louis Post-Dispatch*, Belleville (IL) *News-Democrat,* Edwardsville (IL) Intelligencer, *The Riverbender* (IL) and EdGlen.com (IL).

Posting videos and photos from both special events across social platforms, we gained additional exposure on Facebook, Instagram, and other social channels.

In all, the campaign reached a combined potential audience of 2.9 million.

It enabled the client to convey his messaging as desired and successfully build the brand for the website and future show.

The Jackie Robinson contracts reminded everyone of the great effort Robinson took to break the color barrier in Major League Baseball. On a much lesser scale the PR campaign broke a speed barrier for high intensity action and fast results.

CAMPAIGN TAKEAWAYS

- **Expertise and Experience**
  The importance of high-level visibility within a niche audience generated results for both the client and our agency. The client saw our work online, and learned about our expertise in sports-related PR. It was a good fit.
- **Flexibility**
  We were fortunate to have the personnel available to quickly build and execute campaign.
- **Media Training**
  The client commanded the microphone and generated interviews that went well past the standard allotted time. This provided better rapport with the interviewer, more airtime, and an exceptional brand building experience.

Campaign #11
SARS Wars

Long before the most recent pandemic of 2020, there was SARS (severe acute respiratory syndrome). First identified at the end of February 2003, it is a viral respiratory disease caused by a SARS-associated virus.

The disease is airborne and can spread through small droplets of saliva in a similar way to a cold or influenza. It was discovered during an outbreak in China and spread to four other countries.

It was the first severe and readily transmissible new disease to emerge in the 21st century and showed a clear capacity to spread along the routes of international air travel.

Many medical professionals and scientists were concerned it could spread into a worldwide epidemic as visitors traveled to the United States and beyond.

At the time SARS received a large amount of media attention. Stories appeared daily on news broadcasts and in print. Most Americans were worried they could inadvertently contract the disease.

During this time of heightened public concern, our firm had been engaged by a copier and digital products firm named OfficeWare, based in Louisville, KY. We had been working with them for several months, helping them build general branding and awareness throughout their trade area.

OfficeWare's clients were concerned that through the installation of keyboards and other equipment, and their transference from one person to another—they could be susceptible to acquiring the virus.

To allay those fears, OfficeWare created a SARS flu-avoidance kit. It featured wipes, Kleenex, hand sanitizer, and other items in a clear plastic package. The package was attached to a small sheet which featured a colorful graphic of a germ-like character, tips to avoid the flu, and the OfficeWare logo. OfficeWare's sales representatives and technicians would deliver the kits to their clients.

OfficeWare contacted us and asked if they thought the kit had any type of news value. Once I saw a graphic of the kit and the cartoon-like germ character, I knew this was a hit and could generate extensive news coverage.

Strategy
- Pursue national TV and print coverage
- Pursue local TV and radio coverage
- Pursue local print coverage

We contacted all the major news networks. NBC jumped on it and sent a crew to Louisville to interview the OfficeWare manager. The manager's comments and the flu-avoidance kit were part of a two-minute story that evening on the Nightly News.

The kit also generated coverage on Louisville's local news affiliates. The president of OfficeWare was interviewed on several radio stations. The daily newspaper picked up on the story, writing about how the company was featured on the NBC Nightly News.

Impact
The effort generated millions of positive impressions and created a buzz in the Louisville community.

OfficeWare had a dominant share of voice in its space since no other local document technology firm was even mentioned. The media blitz was in line with OfficeWare's branding goals.

Overall, the company gained a strong foothold in the Louisville market and was later sold to the large international conglomerate Konica Minolta.

Monitoring news broadcasts and understanding what stories are resonating with viewers can help you tailor pitches for top tier results, especially when something novel crosses your desk. A germ of an idea can spawn a large public relations effort, and can result in high impact, both locally and nationally.

CAMPAIGN TAKEAWAYS

➢ **Client Buy-In**
OfficeWare had created the kit for their clients and was willing to support any PR effort to promote it.

➢ **Creative Approach**
The graphic of the germ with the package of healthcare products was innovative and different than anything else.

➢ **Timeliness**
The potential spread of the virus was drawing national attention daily. The timing was ideal to create and promote a small solution that could help.

➢ **Story Packaging**
The OfficeWare kit easily fit into the daily rundown of articles and stories discussing the virus.

Campaign #12
Celebrity Driven Success

The right celebrities in the right place can help build traffic and turn an event into one that is truly special.

We learned this through an engagement with an indoor mall in the St. Louis region.

Once a thriving destination before today's strip centers, seasonal outdoor pop-up venues, and food halls, hundreds traveled regularly to enjoy a weekly shopping and dining experience at the mall.

They would visit their favorite shops, dine at one of several on-site eating establishments, or watch a movie in an attached theatre. Some came to simply hang out.

At their peak, malls were located near high population centers and within several miles of each other. The ongoing quest to build foot traffic and generate new customers for mall merchants was highly competitive.

Many shopping centers would attempt to lure new shoppers through the creation of special events. They had vast spaces to house large gatherings and were quick to utilize them. These happenings would typically take place on weekends and near important holiday buying seasons.

As detailed earlier, our firm has a long history of creating and executing all types of events. One of our clients managed and operated several malls. They invited us to create a fun bash that would build traffic at one their shopping centers in St. Louis' South County.

We were charged with not only promoting it through a variety of PR strategies—but also creating and producing it.

Strategy

Conferring with mall management, we learned the area had a strong focus on sports.

Our goal became to build an event with a sports theme.

Baseball trading card shows were very much in vogue at the time. It enabled sellers of rare cards to turn their prized cardboard into cash. It gave buyers the opportunity to pick up a vintage collectible that could later increase its value and potentially be sold for a handsome profit.

I had attended several baseball card shows in the past and had come to know several collectors. They connected me with those collectors anxious to display their cards and sports memorabilia.

We were able to put together a nice roster of trading card sellers. They agreed to display their wares at tables setup throughout the mall. To ensure a large turnout, we asked the mall manager to set aside some of their budget for a player appearance.

Celebrities help draw the largest crowds—then and now. A special event highlighted by a celebrity appearance can be a motivating force to build traffic for any retailer or customer appreciation event.

Through connections with the St. Louis Cardinals, we were able to secure a visit from Tom Pagnozzi, then a Cardinal's catcher.

Pagnozzi would attend the event, sit at a table, sign autographs, and pose for photos. His presence would provide the cherry on the sundae that would all but guarantee a large turnout.

Back then there was no internet. No social media such as Facebook, Instagram, or TikTok. All promotion would take place working with traditional media.

This included:
- Radio interviews
- Ads in local publications
- Mentions on radio and TV
- Posters at the mall
- Flyers at baseball and trading card shops
- Encouraging collectors to invite their friends to the event
- Additional mall promotion

The media relations helped create a buzz for card enthusiasts, shoppers, and sports fans.

Impact

Hundreds attended the event. Pagnozzi's appearance had the intended impact. Many waited lengthy periods of time to secure an autograph and photo with the Cardinal star.

A few newspaper reporters attended the event and took photos. The enthusiastic fans created their own photo opportunities with excellent visuals for additional post-event publicity. Today many of those photos would appear as selfies on Facebook, Instagram, and other forms of social media.

Traffic was brisk at the baseball card display tables. Mall merchants enjoyed higher shop visits than on a typical Saturday—and greater sales. The event helped enhance the mall's brand and merchant enthusiasm. Based upon its success, mall management asked us to produce another similar event. This one would feature a player from the St. Louis Blues hockey team.

Many malls have ceased to exist. Soon, they may become all but extinct. While the building itself provides a sense of community and entertainment, those things still exist—they've just shifted to a different venue. No matter the arena, knowing your audience and what motivates them helps align the experience with your message in powerful ways.

CAMPAIGN TAKEAWAYS

➢ **Enthusiastic Client**
The mall was excited to create a special event and budget PR and branding dollars to support it.

➢ **Customer Knowledge**
The mall had extensive marketing data on their clientele and realized a sports-related event would be a big draw.

➢ **Celebrity Appearance**
In a sports crazed town, the appearance of the Cardinal catcher was a large draw. Celebrity appearances can generate traffic and buzz no matter the era.

➢ **Agency Knowledge and Topic Awareness**
We were highly aware of the local interest in sports memorabilia and had the expertise to create and produce a successful event.

Campaign #13
Barks & Bites

The job of the PR pro is to get the dog to bark properly. The job of the business is to get it to bite.

I once heard an old adage in the PR business. If you want press coverage, focus on babies and dogs. I never got involved with any campaigns related to infants, but I can bark about our experience with pets.

We were engaged to build the brand for a dog kennel in west St. Louis County. The kennel had a unique selling proposition—the owners lived on the premises.

The family had a large living area above the kennels. The walls were soundproofed for minimal noise. Of course, they had a staff and systems in place should something untoward happen. The idea was that the owners were always onsite to ensure the safety of one's beloved pet. The kennel had been in existence for several years and the owner was ready to grow the number of guests. The goal was to raise brand awareness by emphasizing compassionate, round-the-clock monitored care.

Strategy

The focus would be on advertising and earned media. Our team designed several ads and combined it with efforts to secure TV coverage, newspaper articles, and interviews the client doesn't pay for. As mentioned earlier, earned media provides an indirect third-party endorsement of the business.

In discussions with the kennel, we realized that most people boarded their pet when they traveled. They wanted to leave their pets in good hands, confident their cherished pet would enjoy a pleasurable one or two week stay.

At the time, the Sunday newspaper had a robust travel section. Ads were created to run specifically in those pages. While the ads provided some branding and increased reservations for the kennel, they decided to budget dollars for television advertising for more impact.

The TV ads performed better than the print.

Media relations not only focused on the compassionate care the kennel provided, but also the owner's long family history in the kennel business. Compelling print stories ran in the *St. Louis Post-Dispatch* and other area newspapers.

We were even able to generate a few impactful TV stories on the network news affiliates. Further TV coverage was secured when the kennel hosted a special training event—building brand awareness while promoting the importance of a well-behaved dog.

Impact

In an era prior to social media, both print and television outreach proved to be effective.

The campaign sparked greater buzz about the kennel. The heartfelt ads and coverage connected pet owners with a safe place to leave their furry family members.

Reservations grew and the facility expanded.

The owners eventually retired and left the operation of the kennel to their son, who continued to grow it into a pet hotel and what is now a luxury pet resort. Recently, it was sold to a national operator of pet related services, and after many years it is no longer a family-run operation.

PR and advertising got the dog barking. The client got the profitable bite.

CAMPAIGN TAKEAWAYS

- **Effective Use of the PESO Model**
  Standard PR terminology today, an all-encompassing approach involving:
  - **P**aid communications (advertising)
  - **E**arned media (the no-charge articles and interviews)
  - **S**hared media (via TV, social and print)
  - **O**wned media (flyers, print newsletters, website, brochures).
- **Impactful Story Lines**
  The differentiation of owners living on-site while caring for pets provided lots of story plotlines.
- **Client Flexibility**
  The owners were open to exploring new ideas. They were able to pivot as necessary and invest the necessary dollars for effective message outreach.

Campaign #14
Legends on Wheels

"Driving a classic is like shaking hands with history."
-- Steve McQueen

Sparkling Chrome. Bold Lines. Signature Look. Classic cars are the legends of the road that aren't just vehicles—they're statements.

I have always admired them. Most are the kind you love to look at, but barring a lottery win, will never be able to afford.

European classic cars are especially intriguing. They call out from across the Atlantic. Some with unmatched styling and design.

Years back, that call came my way. I scraped together every last dime to purchase a pre-owned Jaguar MkX. It looked like a mini Rolls Royce, with leather interior and real wooden components—featuring walnut tables that folded down from the back of the front seats for in-car dining.

It was fun to look at, but unfortunately, the automobile was a lemon. It was difficult and expensive to maintain; my parents and friends urged me to sell it. Luckily, I found a buyer and recouped nearly what I had spent—and then invested that money in a newer American car that was built to drive the road ahead, rather than break down before it got there.

Fast forward several decades.

Years down the road my passion for classic cars came full circle. In 2024, our firm found itself in a competitive pitch, vying for the chance to help Daniel Schmitt & Co. Classic Car Gallery—a St. Louis based classic car dealership—increase their presence in the local market. Unlike most small businesses that start locally and expand nationally, they had a large international clientele, yet only a small percentage of local customers.

The dealership was built on a family tradition of selling luxury classic cars for over half a century. Inspired by his father's passion, Daniel Schmitt launched his own dealership in the late 1980s. Over time, the dealership developed a large clientele of high-end collectors—those who enjoyed ownership of rare and historical automobiles and had the means to add to their collection.

Hundreds of people drove by the dealership every day, but few knew what they sold. Only a handful would stop by to see the inventory of high-end investment grade American and European automobiles—some of which were once owned by celebrities.

This would be an ideal fit for us.

We wasted no time contacting the ownership. Soon after, our firm was invited to visit the luxurious dealership to make our proposal. I enjoyed touring the showrooms and viewing some 100 automobiles from Cadillacs and Ferraris to Porsches and Rolls Royce. In the pitch, I shared my passion for classic, luxury cars and my personal experience of owning a Jaguar.

I showed Schmitt our portfolio of work, including case studies of privately-owned companies with similar revenues and plans for growth. We displayed article placements and pointed out the creative process used to secure media interviews on TV and radio that helped other clients create the right messaging, and build their brand to leverage increased sales.

The dealer was also impressed with the awards our firm had received. Including the annual list of top PR firms, published each year in Small Business Monthly. We had achieved that honor for the past sixteen years in a row. We came to an agreement and earned the business.

The investment in that old Jaguar had finally paid dividends.

As Schmitt's PR firm, our role would be to reach more local potential buyers, add branding and influence to the Schmitt name, and increase interest within the St. Louis community. To date, primary marketing efforts centered on targeted ads in select publications and weekly email newsletters, showcasing the newest vehicle arrivals. These newsletters reached thousands of buyers and potential collectors.

Strategy

Daniel Schmitt's backstory helped us craft a campaign that was built upon his passion for cars and family. A native of St. Louis, Schmitt's father had moved to California and launched a Rolls Royce dealership in Beverly Hills. Schmitt spent many years working in the dealership, gaining firsthand experience in business operations and exposure to exclusive inventory tailored to elite and celebrity clientele. Eventually Schmitt returned to St. Louis and launched his own classic car business with limited funds and a small office.

He built it into a $30 million enterprise.

Schmitt's dramatic growth provided the levers for an exciting campaign. One that would focus on the dealership's rich legacy and foundation, and its dealings with all types of celebrities and their automobiles. We were ready to shift gears and start generating local impact.

Media relations, including social media, would be a key focus to drive excitement for the brand and increase foot traffic.

The campaign focus has included:
- Tours of the six-showroom dealership
- Feature stories on Daniel Schmitt in local business publications
- TV stories on rare or celebrity driven vehicles
- Though not the original intent, national media pick-up on the purchase and sale of select automobiles
- Relationship building with key journalists and bloggers who cover the automotive and classic car space
- Invitations to local car clubs to visit the dealership and utilize the facilities for special events
- Leveraging articles and news on social media

Our agency began by pitching members of the local media. We wanted them to not only write an article about Schmitt, but also get a sense and feel of the dealership. This would allow for not just one article—but for follow-up stories as well.

Print and TV journalists came by the dealership. It produced a "quadfecta" of feature articles on Schmitt in all four local businesses and feature-related publications to include the St. Louis Business Journal, St. Louis Post-Dispatch, St. Louis Magazine (digital version), and Small Business Monthly.

We created additional news releases and pitches to spotlight the arrival of high profile automobiles, many of them once celebrity-owned.

The cars were highly visual and ideal for television coverage.

Local TV news covered a Stutz Bearcat once owned and driven

by Elvis Presley. A Fox TV affiliate ran a major feature story when Schmitt acquired a rare presidential vehicle to sell—a presidential limousine once utilized by Jacqueline Kennedy and Lyndon Johnson. More local television coverage was generated when Schmitt bought a Ferrari once owned and driven by Sylvester Stallone. Yet another vehicle Schmitt purchased was once owned and gifted by Frank Sinatra, and also resulted in TV coverage.

When any high-profile vehicle was sold, it made for another impactful story. We created news releases and pitches as vehicles were purchased and sent those to targeted journalists.

The LBJ limousine was sold to a former corporate CEO in California. The sale generated coverage in *The Detroit Free Press*, MSN, *USA Today*, Yahoo, and other outlets.

Stallone's Ferrari was sold to a movie producer and restaurateur. It resulted in several feature articles with classic car writers.

Impact

We generated links to all articles and TV features and posted and re-posted them on social media channels adding "legs" to each story. These were posted on Facebook, LinkedIn, Instagram, and X.

It created valuable content for those unfamiliar with the Schmitt brand.

In all, brand awareness, local interest, and visitors to the dealership have increased. Schmitt has been highly satisfied with the campaign results, and our relationship continues.

Jay Leno, the TV personality and active automobile collector, once said "Classic cars are not just vehicles, they're rolling history, art, and passion all in one."

Schmitt's PR campaign has brought Leno's statement to light, proving the beauty and value of classic automobiles is not just shared among international moguls, but for *all* collectors—even in St. Louis.

CAMPAIGN TAKEAWAYS

- **Focus on Client Back Story**
  Schmitt's background in his father's Beverly Hills dealership and building a thriving St. Louis business provided a strong foundation for all types of local media coverage.
- **Celebrity Influence**
  In an era of celebrity fandom, cars once owned by A-list celebrities provided additional levers for media relations.
- **Micro-Tailoring of Media Pitches**
  Tailor pitches to each medium and the needs of the key journalist. In Schmitt's campaign, some journalists focused on the mechanics of a vehicle others on celebrity. Research each writer's needs for clues on the approach.
- **Media Chain Value**
  Many local newspapers belong to ownership groups such as Gannett and Hearst. An article in one newspaper can and did appear in another or in other media—the TV feature on the limo was even reworked into a newspaper article.

Part III
Craft Masters: Inside the Toolbox—Insights from the Best in the Business

How did the best in the business get to where they are?

They don't just work in PR, they define it, shape it, elevate it. They're the people behind the brands that people talk about. Generating stories that make the headlines, leading their teams, and developing campaigns that move the needle. Thousands are in the PR business, few are masters of the craft. The individuals highlighted here lead the charge. They are at the top of the PR game, serving as mentors by example and setting the industry standard.

I have been fortunate to cross paths with four high-achieving PR professionals—and honored to interview them. Together, we reflect on what sparked their passion for PR, how they supercharged their game, and the advice they offer to anyone wanting to take their career to the next level.

The Lineup Includes:

- Michael Smart, Michael Smart PR
- Taryn Scher, TK Public Relations
- Natalie Bushaw, Vice-President Integrated Communications, Life Time
- Dave Collett, Executive Vice-President, Weber Shandwick

Note: Some responses have been edited for brevity and clarity.

Michael Smart

"Those who stand out are highly persistent. They are wired not to make excuses."

Michael Smart is the owner and operator of Michael Smart PR in Alpine, Utah, a company specializing in media relations consulting and training. He speaks at industry events, trains corporate teams nationally and globally, and operates his own group of PR professionals who wish to advance their careers called the Inner Circle. Now in his 24th year, Michael has worked with many corporate teams ranging from Salesforce, Aflac, Ally, Zillow, and more, and is recognized as the nation's leading trainer of media relations.

What attracted you to public relations?

I became interested in PR as a student at Brigham Young University (BYU). Originally, I wanted to become a sports center anchor and pursued broadcast journalism. At the same time, I was taking a class in mass communications. The professor of that class had worked in public relations at one of the Bell telephone companies. I found his teachings to be more in-line with my aspirations. Sports announcing seemed rather limiting and I decided to pursue a different path focused on other areas of communication.

How did you launch your career?

Writing was always a focus and while a student at BYU I started freelancing for the Salt Lake City Tribune. They paid by performance, and I was able to garner some nice placements in the paper. Eventually I went to work for them on a full-time basis. It was interesting work but I wanted to do something more encompassing. I thought it would be more exciting to advocate for one organization through mass communications. I contacted the administration department at BYU and was hired to work with their PR staff.

I started with the PR team around 1998 and to learn more about the workings of public relations I attended several conferences put on by industry training organizations like the Public Relations Society of America (PRSA) and Ragan. I noted they had several speakers at each conference.

I thought I could do some speaking as well and earn additional income as I had four children with a stay-at-home wife. I started answering RFPs to speak at various events. BYU offered a month of vacation time and I could use those days for training. Conference planners liked my subject matter and began to hire me. I found I was good at connecting and educating many types of audiences and received high scores from attendees.

Some corporations approached me at these conferences and asked if I would be interested in training their teams on the practice of media relations. I started lining up contracts and the income from my training work began to increase.

Michael Smart PR began to take off and I was able to leave BYU in 2012 and start my own full-time company.

How many professionals have you trained since you started?

Some 10,000 PR pros have attended various aspects of my training. These include corporate teams to individual practitioners just getting started in the industry.

Many have attended through paid engagements at live conferences. Some have attended virtually.

I have trained teams not only in the U.S. but also globally. Those destinations that stand out include Bangkok Thailand, Tokyo, Japan and Geneva, Switzerland.

The Inner Circle, of which I am a member, is an interesting group of hundreds of public relations professionals all wishing to enhance their skills in media relations. How did this idea emerge?

It actually started as a little experiment in 2009. I got 10 or 11 people together and we began discussing key issues in the industry.

We had an awesome response and people began talking about it. It really ramped up around 2014 and is now the primary aspect of my business.

Since you have worked with thousands in the industry, what

separates the really good professionals from the average ones?

Let's start with the average media relations pros. They all have an understanding of how the media works. Most can keep a story interesting working with members of the media and many influencers. The poor ones don't even have this skill.

Meantime those who stand out are highly persistent. They are wired not to make excuses.

For example, say your job is to publicize dish detergent. Many will find it boring. They will send out the same old company stories with mediocre results. Meantime the superstar will take the initiative to look at the company's R&D facility and figure out other forms of coverage. They will leverage their creativity, generate excellent results, and become highly valued. These are the ones that get promoted or get hired by organizations with lots of news, ones where they don't have to continually hunt for story ideas.

Pitching matters. You can make a list of your top ten targets and get ghosted on the first nine. The superstars will go after the tenth contact on their list and land the story when most everyone else would have given up. They may have average skills but are extremely persistent.

PR seems to be changing by the minute. Where do you see the industry heading?

The top media relations professionals will be adept at building relationships with all types of influencers, from all types of outlets.

These include traditional influencers like a reporter at a newspaper such as the Financial Times to someone writing for Substack, to business-to-business influencers to solo media organizations.

I read that former Fox and NBC News host Megyn Kelly has a podcast that generated over 30 million more views in July 2024 on YouTube than either NBC or CBS news properties. These independent types of podcasters have a strong influence with their audience connections.

It will be up to those in the PR industry to connect with these macro influencers and determine how to get their stories and messaging to resonate with their audiences for top line results.

Finally, based on everything you have told us, what do you recommend now for those who wish to pursue a career in public relations.

First I would say any textbook on public relations is now obsolete.

As mentioned earlier, the industry and especially media relations is changing quickly and will continue to do so.

I would recommend young professionals change tactics to reach out to influencers in their targeted space. Reply to journalists but keep track of social posts and respond to those with followings you seek. Monitor bloggers and instagrammers and see if you can connect with micro influencers. The goal is to get on their radar and make yourself a reliable resource. This will be the wave of the future.

POWER MOVES

- The top media relations professionals will be adept at building relationships with all types of influencers, from all types of outlets.
- Reply to journalists, but keep track of social posts and respond to those with followings you seek.
- Monitor bloggers and Instagrammers to see if you can connect with micro influencers. The goal is to get on their radar and make yourself a reliable resource.

Taryn Scher

"Read and watch what the media is writing and talking about, and then formulate story ideas in tune with their readers."

Taryn Scher is the owner of TK PR, in Greenville, South Carolina. The firm has carved a niche as a go-to agency for companies involved with the travel and leisure industry. Scher started the firm in 2008 and is highly recognized for her ability to land top tier media placements with the national media. Her clients appear frequently on network news programs, travel and leisure magazines and major newspapers. TK PR works with convention and visitor organizations, hotels, restaurants, and resorts. Her bright, cheery light-up-the room attitude has earned Scher the nickname The Sparkle Boss.

Let's start by discussing how you found your way into the practice of public relations.

I attended journalism school at the University of Maryland. I was focused on the broadcast track. On graduation I moved to New York. A number of friends had located there to work in the fashion industry.

PR was big there and I saw lots of opportunity. I told my parents I was going to forgo broadcasting and focus on Public Relations. They said well then you have eight weeks to get a job.

I was 22 and really didn't know a thing about public relations. Through some contacts I was able to land a job as an executive assistant with a luxury fashion company. They were an Asian firm that wanted to grow and had entered the U.S. market. I was doing a little bit of everything, including some marketing to assist with whatever they needed.

The company hired a large New York City PR agency specializing in fashion. The agency sent over a team of women who looked good and smelled good, but they really didn't get anything done. Meantime the company was in the process of opening a highly visible three-story store on the corner of 5th Avenue and 53rd Street. Yet there were no stories to support this large opening. The agency was also charging a lot of money. The fee for one month was equivalent to what I was making for five months.

I was confident I could produce better results than the agency. I asked my boss to give me a few months and I would show him what could be done. I spoke to some friends who worked for PR agencies and got a feel for what was going on and what was missing. After a three-month trial period they liked the placements I was able to generate. They terminated the PR firm, and I got promoted. I found I really liked digging in, writing and developing story ideas. I became their head of PR and worked there for another a year and a half.

Meantime my husband to-be was studying medicine. He got an internship in Greenville and we planned to head South.

In 2007, well before remote work was even a consideration, I told my boss that I could do the job from Greenville. He agreed but said I could no longer be an employee. He said you need to have your own business and we will be your client.

How did you learn the nuances of public relations without any training?

Everything I learned is basically self-taught. I didn't know much about PR at the University of Maryland and at the time there wasn't much in general for public relations courses on the internet.

About all I had known about public relations was from watching Samanatha Jones on *Sex In The City*.

I started taking journalists to lunch and got a better understanding of what they needed and how to position a story.

I did research and lots of homework and figured out how to create impactful story ideas.

I didn't like the cookie cutter approach used by some large agencies so I created my own rules of PR. I borrowed on what my parents taught me, treat everyone the way you would like to be treated.

It began to pay off and would eventually lead to many

placements with top tier media organizations.

How did you expand your agency?

We had moved to Greenville and I had the fashion company as a client. I never thought about adding additional clientele. Then I spoke to a public relations friend who said legally there was nothing preventing you from taking on more companies. She also said she could use some help with a project, a large food and wine festival in Napa Valley in California. She asked if I would be willing to do some freelance work.

I told her I didn't know anything about the wine industry, but I would be willing to do whatever they needed. She said don't worry about it. I'll give you the information you need. Just do what you're good at.

I did tons of research and when I eventually got to Napa I could speak their language.

The vibe was great. More laid back than the fast-paced fashion industry. Everyone eating and drinking and having a good time.

I knew it was going to be my future. So now I had two clients, one in fashion, one in food and wine.

Meantime we were still new to Greenville and didn't have many friends. I was working from home and met a woman on the board of the Greenville Visitors and Convention Center.

She said they were in the process of putting on their own food and wine festival and needed some publicity and promotion. They really didn't have a budget but asked if I could help.

I volunteered thinking I would meet a lot of people in the area. It turned out to be the best decision I could make.

The event was successful, and I made numerous contacts. Many of those connections were board members and local decision makers. It resulted in new business opportunities.

Through those efforts I was invited to work for the Greenville Convention and Visitors Bureau. The goal was to attract weekend visitors to the area.

Over time I secured a lot of national exposure for Greenville and brought all types of people to the region, increasing patrons for hotels and restaurants.

The organization and its budget have grown considerably and today we not only handle public relations for what is now VisitGreenvilleSC but several other branding initiatives.

How has TK PR built a client base that extends far beyond Greenville?

Leaders in other cities saw what we were doing in Greenville and for other clients. They noticed all the national placements we were generating like the Today Show, The New York Times, and Southern Living, and wanted similar campaigns to help build tourism in their region.

The phones began ringing and we were invited to meet with decision makers in several other markets.

Recently we began working with Macon, Georgia. The area and approach reminded me a lot of what Greenville looked like when we arrived in 2007. They have a lot of great attributes to promote. The same holds true for Sandy Springs, Georgia near Atlanta whom we have also added to our list of clients.

We don't take on everyone who calls. I am hands-on so overall we have limited bandwidth. That is why we are very selective about what types of clients we work with. Our focus is purely travel and leisure, and those seeking national exposure. We get inquiries all the time from all types of businesses wishing to engage our services.

It may not be the best business decision, but we turn down about 90% of the people who contact us.

What also differentiates us is unlike most agencies we focus on quality of story placements not quantity. Then we help clients generate more legs from a story when they get a big placement.

We have also expanded our capabilities where we are not only involved in media relations but also branding and marketing communications.

Over time we have developed metrics in line with an organization's KPIs and data so they can see all the value of the results we generate.

Recently we sponsored the Travel and Leisure PR Conference put on by the Public Relations Society of America. Around 300 PR professionals attended. I got to showcase our highlight reel video of national media placements. It created quite a buzz and a lot of chatter. I knew then we had arrived and were a player in the space usually dominated by huge agencies.

Though we are small, when it comes to the travel and leisure industry TK PR simply crushes it.

Recently you added to your staff. What do you look for in a new hire?

I look for that unicorn, that special person who has the sparkle attitude to do the hard work and become successful.

I love developing story ideas and working with journalists and look for the same zest from anyone who wants to work here.

It's not an easy job. You have to spend the time, do the digging, read and watch what the media is writing and talking about, and then formulate story ideas in tune with their readers. We can give someone the tools and teach them the mechanics, but their attitude is crucial.

Recently I got a resume from a local college grad whom I was considering for employment. Suddenly I got four phone calls from people in Greenville saying I must hire her. This was even before she came in for an interview. Even though she was young they said she had the special qualities that make her standout from the crowd.

Once I interviewed her I knew they were right. Now she is the newest member of our team.

Finally, you have developed this persona as The Sparkle Boss. How did that originate?

Around five years ago I was looking to develop my own brand and web site and started looking at some photographs.

I noticed my dorm room had different types of sparkles along the walls.

I'm known to be outgoing with an uplifting personality. Some even say I light up the room when I come in. Someone called me "Sparkles" so, I went with it.

I started wearing a sparkly blazer or shoes when I went to meetings. It really helped me stand out from the crowd.

It worked so well that people started sending me all types of gifts with sparkles on them.

It's become so engrained that when I speak at an event and I'm not wearing a sparkly piece of clothing they ask me about it.

The Sparkle Boss has been a nice brand identity, a visual leave-behind people don't forget.

POWER MOVES

- Create your own PR rules—don't use the cookie cutter approach many large agencies use.
- Be selective with clients. TK PR's focus is purely travel and leisure, and those seeking national exposure.
- Hire "unicorns", that special person who has the sparkle attitude to do the hard work and become successful.

Natalie Bushaw

"PR is about building relationships and good communication skills are a must."

Natalie Bushaw is the Vice-President of Integrated Communications at Life Time, one of the nation's leading fitness and lifestyle brands. She has had an extensive career working in public relations with a large national retail company, a media company that produced Delta's Sky magazine, and a company that sold fitness equipment. Natalie manages a team of three PR professionals and supervises the company's work with national and regional agencies. Her work has helped Life Time achieve leading brand awareness among fitness and lifestyle centers nationwide with nearly 1.5 individual members in some 180 centers. Life Time is a public company and is traded on the New York Stock Exchange.

You have had a vast career in public relations working with a variety of companies. How did it all begin?

Early on I wanted to be a sports announcer. I had what it took, but I became worried I would be stuck in my hometown in Austin, Minnesota. I got a degree in mass communications with an emphasis on advertising and public relations.

I have a very outgoing personality and love to meet and connect with other people. A small public relations firm in the Minneapolis area brought me in as an account executive. From there I joined Dayton Hudson Corporation, a large conglomerate, that included Marshall Fields, Target and others, as a senior manager and publicist. Eventually I would become Director of Public Relations for Macy's North/Marshall Fields and its 63 stores.

Then I transitioned to handle marketing communications for the company that produced the Delta Sky magazine that reached 13 million passengers each month. The industry changed and I applied for a position with Life Time. I was working out at one of their facilities and heard about an opening. I loved everything they were doing and got the position. They brought me on in 2013 and I have been there ever since.

How have your responsibilities grown at Life Time?

I started as Director of Media Relations to help build the brand. I wanted to spread the word about everything going on at the company and promote a healthy lifestyle. I was responsible to make sure Life Time received great media coverage for its brand, business, and programs. I worked closely with club leadership, executive leadership and events.

In 2017 I was promoted to Senior Director Public Relations & Internal Communications. We were experiencing huge growth and I was leading a team that created and executed communications strategies that motivated and inspired our entire 30,000 team members. We also wanted to provide media and influencers with great content about Life Time. In 2021, I became Vice President of Public Relations and Corporate Communications. Today I lead our PR team, work with our external PR agency of record, coordinate activity with several regional public relations firms and I am heavily involved in corporate communications strategy and planning.

What does your typical day entail?

A big part is working with businesses inside Life Time to make sure we are really generating impactful coverage. We will be launching our health products like proteins, vitamins and supplements and I am working with related press releases and events regarding that.

Our CEO was asked recently to speak on a panel with Fast Company magazine and I was in New York for that event. We had a situation in St. Louis with one of our clubs that was political and generated a lot of media attention. I had attended a separate event in New York, got back to the office the next day, and then had to head to St. Louis to work with the team in that market. I also work with our national agency on national media, and our in-house team, which is more focused on local media. Leadership development is part of it with our young team. Then I sometimes get involved with club leaders on certain issues where PR may play a role.

What's been your greatest accomplishment at life time?
I would start with playing a role in the transition we made from a private to a public company—it was really fantastic. Orchestrating a lot of the communications in the process was something special.

Also, the way we responded and dealt with the global pandemic was a great learning experience and made our team stronger. In one day, we had to shut down all our clubs. Leading the company through that with the right mix of communications is something I am proud of. Meanwhile, the media was grabbing on to all the workout at home fitness equipment and talking about it incessantly. But we still needed to create positive media coverage. We focused more on our brand and lifestyle, and not just about Life Time as a gym. It helped create many valuable media relationships with top tier media. When the pandemic ended, we came out of it a lot stronger from a brand perspective and positioned Life Time as a more upscale experience. It's all the result of the work we have been doing with the media. I am so proud of our team and the way we worked through those challenges.

You currently manage a small internal PR team. What attributes do you seek when making a new hire?
I look for those who have an engaging personality. They must exude confidence and be able to carry on a conversation. PR is about building relationships and good communication skills are a must. In our case they must also be dedicated to living a healthy lifestyle and have a thorough understanding of our brand.

Finally, I would lean towards individuals who understand the big picture of where the industry is headed. It is not just about communications but understanding the nuances of the brand, business, and economic trends.

What advice do you have for those recent graduates who wish to work in public relations?
Media relations is most of our focus so they need to read their local newspapers, watch TV news, and listen to the radio to learn what stories they are telling to match the needs of their client or business.

Social media is also a big part of everything we do. I

would encourage them to not only educate themselves on social media, but also search engine optimization and everything related to it.

Watch online tutorials and subscribe to newsletters that you trust.

They should also learn about KPIs and what types of stories and PR activities actually move the needle and help the business grow.

Finally, they should be acquainted with the PESO model that involves various aspects of the communications plan, and how it all interacts. This includes paid media, earned media (not bought), shared media along social channels, and owned media—that which the brand has full control over such as a website, newsletter, and blog.

Any recommendations for those who have been in the industry for a while and want to take their career to the next level?

I would tell them to "look in." They need to look at themselves and determine if they are where they need to be. If they wish to move up the ladder or assume a leadership role, they should ask questions and get feedback about what they need to do to expand their role. They can sign up for coursework and other ways to enhance their knowledge.

Secondly, they need to "look out." What have you done and what you could do more of. Find a mentor or pay for a service that will help them fill in the gaps and offer advice. Look for mentors who have already achieved whatever goals you seek and spend time with them to enhance your skills for advancement.

Finally, I hold dear what a manager told me when I worked for a radio station. Four words: "ask for the sale." If you believe in something you truly want to do ask for it. If you don't ask you will never get it. Be confident and make sure you have the stuff to back it up.

POWER MOVES

> ➢ Educate yourself on social media and search engine optimization—and everything related to it.
> ➢ Warch online tutorials and subscribe to newsletters.
> ➢ Ask for the sale—if you don't ask, you will never get it.

Dave Collett

"PR pros need to abide by a code and follow it. In a world of mixed messaging, it will help build the value we can bring to the client."

Dave Collett is Executive VP/Markets Leader with Weber Shandwick, an international public relations firm based in New York. Dave manages the company's St. Louis office and its team of 40 public relations professionals and is a member of the firm's senior corporate communications practice. Collett has risen through the ranks at Weber and at one time not only managed the St. Louis office but the Minneapolis branch as well. He and his team work with a number of well-known brands such as Kellenova (formerly Kellogg), AB InBev, Mars, Coca Cola and Bayer. In all Dave has more than 25 years of experience guiding high-profile media and marketing initiatives for businesses, brands and causes from private equity-backed start-ups to the Fortune 100.

You have enjoyed great success in the public relations industry, was PR your first career choice?

Originally, I was thinking about becoming a lawyer. I was studying at Northeast Missouri State (now Truman State) and had a strong interest in not only law but business. I took a class in public relations and found it combined a lot of the areas I liked such as corporate communications and writing. It was a great fit. I spent some time writing for the school newspaper and creating stories. Then I was able to secure an internship at FleishmanHillard in St. Louis. It was there that I realized I had found my professional home.

How did your career path lead to Weber Shandwick?

Upon graduation I was anxious to leverage my internship and work full time at Fleishman. Unfortunately, at the time they didn't have any openings. They did refer me to the public relations team at McDonnell Douglas as they were transitioning to become Boeing. I was hired by McDonnell Douglas and did a little of everything from general PR to writing to leading site tours.

Soon thereafter, I answered a blind ad in the newspaper for a company seeking an entry-level PR person. Ironically it turned out it was FleishmanHillard. I secured an interview and got the job. I spent seven years at Fleishman and became a vice-president. The key client I was working with moved from Fleishman to Weber Shandwick. Weber contacted me and asked if I was willing to switch to work with the client. We came to terms, and I started there also as a VP.

You have had a number of roles at Weber—can you give us some highlights?

I oversaw a global account which required me to go to New York every week and take part in their corporate communications. I eventually became a senior vice-president and global relationship account lead. Then I was appointed to lead the St. Louis office as its general manager and head our team of some 40 professionals. One thing we do at Weber is network and discuss client strategies nationally among our leading group of pros in some 12 offices. We connect weekly and I am involved in that process.

As technology such as AI continues to affect the PR industry, how do you stay atop industry trends and practices?

I have never been afraid to test new technologies and see how we can apply them to improve our operation. Early on when the Internet was first gaining traction, I was among the first in the Fleishman office to experiment and determine how to leverage it to make our jobs more efficient. I showed others how they could search for information online rather than taking the time to do it all manually. It's become my superpower.

Today, what helps me maintain a leading-edge approach is through a course I teach at Washington University in St. Louis. It's called Strategic Integrated Communications. It requires students to plan a campaign from scratch doing research, budgeting, ideas, and execution from start to finish. I use examples of companies taking a novel approach in communications, keeping our client work totally separate from any classroom discussion. Though I don't teach it every semester, everything is constantly evolving with artificial intelligence, tech disruption, and its effect on the media, for example. Doing the research and presenting it helps me stay on top of the game.

What advice can you provide for recent college graduates or young professionals who wish to work at a large international agency like Weber Shandwick?
First let me say with regards to the St. Louis office, the area punches above its weight when it comes to its place in the PR landscape. Some of this is due to Fleishman's home office located in the market. There are also good area colleges with solid communications programs. The University of Missouri of course has its renowned journalism school. Other schools such as St. Louis University, Southern Illinois University, and Truman State are all on our radar for qualified potential hires or internships.

Many of the colleges have PR programs where students can work in a public relations agency. It gives them hands-on experience of what it will be like to research, plan and work in the industry. It gives them real world insights and helps them prepare for their careers.

I also encourage students to embrace new tech and learn about it. If you grew up with it you have an advantage and you can lead the way. Understand what a story is and what it isn't. You're going to grow the most if you stay curious and continually learn new skills.

That all being said, the PR business is getting more complicated, and we don't hire as many interns as we have in the past. We look for people who have three, five, or ten years of experience. We like for them to have done some things but still have plenty of room for growth.

What I really like are those with a nose for news. Since media relations is still a large part of what we do, I look for those who go beyond the obvious. They are willing to dig deep into complicated and dense subjects, find a story, and turn it into news. Like looking for a needle in a haystack. That ability can help separate them from the pack.

You talk about embracing new technology. What do you envision for the future of public relations?

AI will certainly be a key part of the future. It will determine how people curate information. There is an upside for PR with ChatGPT and what users will get with earned media. Engaging with young audiences will also be important. A question that will need to be answered is what role TikTok will play. Some communications will be real, some fake. Some savvy from users will be required to separate fact from fiction. All that will require some expertise and counseling from PR firms as to how client messages are coming across AI. There is a feeling to be bullish about it with earned media and how it will be used. Technology keeps getting better and better. It will be interesting to see where that leads in 2-5 years.

One area that needs attention is the industry's measurement concepts. There are lots of systems and calculations, but not a normally accepted model like in advertising. A business can buy ads online and determine how much they have to spend to generate a certain number of responses and a certain number of purchases. They understand what they're spending and what kind of return they will receive. We don't have that in PR.

Ethics is another area that deserves more industry focus. PR pros need to abide by a code and follow it. In a world of mixed messaging, it will help build the value we can bring to the client.

Finally, you have been at Weber for over two decades. What are you most proud of?

I'm most proud of the people I've helped recruit and bring into Weber Shandwick, as well as helping connect people in transition to their next big thing. I think that gives me as much personal satisfaction as anything I've done in my career. I always say, if you can get the people part right, the rest is a lot easier.

POWER MOVES

- Dig deep into complicated and dense subjects, find a story, and turn it into news.
- New students should look for a college that now only has a PR program but offers the opportunity to work at a PR agency.
- Stay curious and continually learn new skills.

Elements for Success: The PR Campaign Top 10

HAVE A GREAT STORY TO TELL

This is key. If you don't have anything interesting for the media, why would they cover it? The skill in this is to identify the story idea and then work with people in the company to flush out the specifics and give it some personality to make it appetizing for the media.

DETERMINE WHAT TOOLS YOU WILL NEED TO COMMUNICATE YOUR STORY

Sure, everyone needs a news release or pitch letter—but what other tools will help sell your story? This could be a video, infographic, white paper, or research that elevates your pitch and helps you stand out from the crowd. Visuals and graphics sell well with today's audience.

RESEARCH YOUR TARGETED MEDIA BEFORE SENDING

Analyze your targeted publications or TV stations and see if they run stories similar to those you are pitching. If your story idea is business oriented it will be difficult to sell it to a consumer-related publication. Read and watch and see if your story idea makes sense for the media you are targeting.

WRITE WELL

You need to communicate your pitch in an email. This needs to be done in simple, concise, but interesting sentences. Busy journalists don't have time to read elongated pitches and releases that don't get to the point. Make sure you write in a style that sells your story—or find someone who can.

CREATE A GOOD EMAIL HEADLINE

Since most communication is done by email, you need to make your subject line interesting, so it stands out from the crowd. Instead of "Man Finds Feast At Area Hamburger Restaurant" make it:

"Man Breaks Record, Eats 12 Hamburgers in 5 Minutes—Sets New Record. Why Did He Do It?"

PREP AND PREPARE

Nothing is worse than having an unprepared interviewee. Whether it is a CEO or someone else in the organization, determine what you wish to communicate in advance. Write it out and ensure they stay on point.

REHEARSE AND ROLE PLAY

Speaking to a reporter on the phone is one thing, doing a TV interview is another. Rehearse in advance and role play with one person playing the interviewer. For TV, using a studio-like setting with a microphone and bright lights is always good training.

DRESS APPROPRIATELY

You are the "brand." If you are going to be on TV or in a photograph for an article, dress how you want people to perceive your brand. A t-shirt and tattered jeans usually won't cut it if you head a large company, or even a small one for that matter. You want viewers to have positive images of doing business with your firm.

LEVERAGE YOUR STORY AND GIVE IT "LEGS"

One method for gaining additional media coverage from one story is to leverage it for another. For example, when one of our clients was on the NBC Nightly News we contacted the local newspaper and told them about it. They had a local gossip type column and ran a story that our client was on network television.

AMPLIFY YOUR NEWS ON SOCIAL MEDIA

You can reach thousands more by sending out your article or TV story on social media. You can link it to your corporate or personal sites. In many cases your followers and friends may like it and re-post it. This way you generate thousands of more views with just a little effort.

For the Road Ahead

In the end, I will leave you with the greatest lesson as you pursue excellence in PR and in life.

"Don't Quit" by Edgar Alan Guest

When things go wrong, as they sometimes will,
when the road you're trudging seems all uphill,
when the funds are low and the debts are high,
and you want to smile but you have to sigh,
when care is pressing you down a bit - rest if you must, but don't you quit.

Life is queer with its twists and turns.
As everyone of us sometimes learns.
And many a fellow turns about when he might have won had he stuck it out.
Don't give up though the pace seems slow - you may succeed with another blow.
Often the goal is nearer than it seems to a faint and faltering man;

Often the struggler has given up when he might have captured the victor's cup;
and he learned too late when the night came down,
how close he was to the golden crown.

Success is failure turned inside out - the silver tint of the clouds of doubt,
and you never can tell how close you are,
it may be near when it seems afar;
so stick to the fight when you're hardest hit — it's when things seem worst, you must not quit.

Resource Guide:
Featured Companies & Helpful Links

Featured Links

Amini's Home, Rugs And Game Room
  Chesterfield, MO
  www.aminis.com

Birch Telecom
  Acquired by Fusion Connect in 2018
  www.fusionconnect.com

Brian Tracy International
  www.briantracy.com

Cohen Woodworking
  www.Cohenwoodworking.com

The Common Cents Show – Podcast
  Garrett Reed
  www.commoncentsthepodcast.com

The DESCO Group
  www.descogroup.com

Eric Thomas, Motivational Speaker
  www.ericthomas.com

H.F. Epstein Hebrew Academy
  University City, Missouri
  www.eha.org

Integrated Communications at Life Time
  Natalie Bushaw, Vice-President
  www.lifetime.life

Michael Smart PR
  Michael Smart, Owner & Operator
  Alpine, Utah
  www.michaelsmartpr.com

Northwestern Mutual-St. Louis
  www.northwesternmutual.com

Original Jeeps, Paul Bruno
  www.originaljeeps.com

TK PR
   Taryn Scher, Owner
   Greenville, South Carolina
   www.tkpublicrelations.com
ThrottleNet
   www.throttlenet.com
Tony Robbins
   www.tonyrobbins.com
Weber Shandwick
   Dave Collett, Executive VP/Markets Leader
   www.webershandwick.com

Helpful Links

Kantar BrandZ's 2025 Most Valuable Global Brands Report
   www.kantar.com
Muck Rack
   www.muckrack.com
Paine Publishing – Katie Delahaye Paine
   www.painepublishing.com
Public Relations Society of America, PRSA
   www.prsa.org
StoryBrand
   www.Storybrand.com

About Steve Turner

Steve Turner is the Managing Principal of Solomon Turner, Inc., an award-winning public relations agency in a St. Louis, MO. A firm he and his partner, Shelly Solomon, founded in 1990.

A graduate of the University of Missouri and its school of Journalism, Turner began his career as a news and sports announcer. He eventually transitioned into advertising sales and radio station management. Turner's creative approach to branding and campaign management provided the impetus to launch his own public relations agency in St. Louis. He merged with S. Solomon & Associates, an advertising agency, and formed Solomon Turner PR—now in its third decade.

Turner's firm provides public relations counseling and campaign execution for businesses and organizations on a national, regional, and local basis. Clients span industries ranging from automotive and construction to healthcare, high-tech, retail, sports, and telecommunications. The firm has been named one of the top PR firms in St. Louis for 17 years in a row by *Small Business Monthly*.

Turner has worked with many companies such as Anthony (Tony) Robbins Seminars, Brian Tracy, Coldwell Banker, Northwestern Mutual, and Veterans Home Care. A frequent media contributor, he has been quoted and/or featured in the Associated Press, *Forbes*, Everything PR, Industry Leaders, *Parade*, PR Week, Public Relations Society of America, *Small Business Monthly*, and *The Wall Street Journal*. Turner was named a Rockstar Publicist by *Authority Magazine* available on Medium.com, and has appeared on TV, radio, and podcasts.

PR THAT WORKS builds on the successful strategies, campaigns, and thought processes Steve has learned from a PR career spanning over 30 years. To learn more visit: https://getprthatworks.com or https://solomonturner.com.

www.ingramcontent.com/pod-product-compliance
Lightning Source LLC
Chambersburg PA
CBHW050900160426
43194CB00011B/2225